101 WAYS

to F$$k up

YOUR

ESTATE

Don't $$k it up! Peggy Hoyt

PEGGY R. HOYT, J.D., M.B.A.

Peggy R. Hoyt -- 1st ed.

ISBN: 978-1-954757-12-7

The Publisher has strived to be as accurate and complete as possible in the creation of this book.

This book is not intended for use as a legal, business, accounting, or financial advice source. All readers are advised to seek the services of competent professionals in legal, business, accounting, and finance fields.

Like anything else in life, there are no guarantees of income or results in practical advice books. Readers are cautioned to rely on their judgment about their individual circumstances to act accordingly.

While all attempts have been made to verify information provided in this publication, the Publisher assumes no responsibility for errors, omissions, or contrary interpretation of the subject matter herein. Any perceived slights of specific persons, peoples, or organizations are unintentional.

Contents

INTRODUCTION

Why did I write a book called "101 Ways to F$$k Up Your Estate?" It's because I've spent most of the last half-century of my life shaking my head at the devastating things people do when it comes to one of the most important planning arenas in their life. Most of the events described in this book could have been avoided with three legal documents - a Last Will, a Durable Financial Power of Attorney and/or a Prenuptial Agreement; and a strong relationship with a legal professional they know and trust.

I hope you don't take offense to the title of the book. I feel like I'm old enough to be blunt, and I had to find a way to get your attention. I hope I have. I also hope you will enjoy reading this book and come away with some tips that will save you (and your family) from making some of the same mistakes.

Most people spend more time planning a single vacation than they do planning the disposition and control of all of their assets - everything they have spent their entire life earning, investing, and preserving. And, if you love your family at all, you'd think you'd want to make life easier, not harder for them. Yet, somehow we don't. We say we want to make things easier, but then we do not take the necessary steps to actually make it all happen. Sometimes this is because it's too hard, too expensive, or too overwhelming. Sometimes it's the "round to it" that we never get around to. Sometimes we fear what we don't know and simply stick our heads in the sand.

Some of you have done your estate planning, and I applaud you. However, if it has been more than five years since you've had a thorough review of your legal estate plan and how it integrates with your financial plan, then you likely have committed one or more of the mistakes outlined in this book. Life happens fast. Review your estate plan each year when you do your taxes to see if any changes in your life or your legacy might affect your plan.

The book was only supposed to have 101 hints, hence the title. However, once I got started, the list just kept growing, and rather than leave something out that might be important, I just kept writing. I hope you will indulge me. I also hope you will find one or more of these suggestions that will make a difference in your life or the life of your family. Ultimately, I hope it will make things easier. At least you've been warned.

Americans are optimistic. We believe we aren't going to die, and we are all going to win the lottery! Don't believe me? Listen to the way people talk. A person will say, "If I die," and "When I win the lottery." I met a 93-year-old lady the other day - she was just getting around to her planning and was inspired by the loss of her husband of 65 years. She said, "We didn't think we were going to live forever; we just didn't think we were going to die!" I believe this sums it up for most of us. We are all going to die someday, just not today.

The years 2020 and 2021 have certainly changed the way many people view death and the inevitability of death. Our estate planning and elder law firm has never been busier. Existing clients are updating their estate planning. New clients are anxious to get their planning done. People are finally paying attention.

And, many of us have lost loved family members, either to disease, accident, or old age. The administration of a loved one's estate is emotional, time-consuming, and sometimes without financial reward. Hopefully, you can spare your family from some of the negative outcomes I've seen.

I'm not perfect, but at least I take my own advice. I always have. I'm surprised how many professionals don't. When I was a financial advisor (in my first career), I kept my financial house in order. I saved a percentage of my paycheck for an emergency fund. I dollar-cost averaged my mutual fund investments with dividend reinvestment. I paid myself first, so I was always saving. I bought life insurance, disability insurance, long-term care insurance, and umbrella insurance for excess liability. I had my eye on my financial future.

As an estate planning lawyer, I keep my estate plan updated and relevant to my current family and financial situation. I make changes when the law changes or when I get smarter. I review my beneficiary designations regularly. I have a Pet Trust for the benefit of my pets. I have trusts for adult children to provide them with asset and divorce protection. I walk my talk.

Does that mean I won't possibly someday die when the last "i" isn't dotted and the last "t" crossed? "No," but I will definitely have made my best effort. That's all I'm asking you to do too. Hope is not a plan. Do the best you can for the people you love.

CHAPTER ONE

Tips for Everybody

The tips included in this section apply universally to everyone regarding estate planning and estate administration. As a result, this is the most extensive section of the book and addresses most estate planning concerns. Subsequent sections will address issues specific to smaller groups of individuals with unique or niche planning concerns.

1 Think you don't need an estate plan.

Everyone has an estate plan, whether they know it or not. The state where you live has created one for you. These laws are called intestacy statutes. When you die without a will (no estate plan), the intestacy statutes determine how your estate will be distributed. Depending on where you live and how much you like your family, you may get a result you are completely unprepared for. This falls under the category of "how people you don't even like

1

can inherit your estate." If you are estranged from your spouse or children and die without a will, they will still be entitled to your estate. If you have no spouse or children, then your parents or your siblings will inherit your estate.

Contrary to common belief, the state doesn't get your money and property when you have no will. That only happens when you die without a will, and you don't have anyone left you are related to. The legal term for this predicament is "escheat." Your estate *escheats* to the state. This doesn't happen very often because most people have living relatives, although they may be quite distant or even undesirable. This is how people in soap operas inherit riches from an uncle they never knew they had.

Sometimes people don't plan because they think they don't have an "estate." Like an estate plan, everyone has an estate. It's everything you own, everything you control, and everything your name is on. It might also be the proceeds from a lawsuit that results in your injury or death. There are lots of ways people end up with an estate they didn't count on.

2 Rely on wishful thinking as an estate plan.

I'm surprised by the number of times clients have told me they don't need an estate plan because they told their family what they want and believe their family will abide by their wishes. This is feel-good thinking. Take it from me, when there is money involved, the intentions of even our most trusted family members can change on a dime.

Also, what you wish for may not be consistent with the legal outcome of your decisions. I've argued with more than one mother who insisted her children would do the right thing and share with one another in the event of her death. However, I know this is not true because many litigators making a ton of money prove these moms wrong.

3 **Only create a Last Will.**
So, you've bought into the idea that you need a Last Will. Good for you. However, if that's all you've done, you haven't done enough. What happens if you become mentally disabled? A Last Will doesn't become effective until you die. If you are alive but mentally disabled, you may very well end up in guardianship court as an unwilling participant in a guardianship proceeding. You could have prevented that expensive, time-consuming, intrusive proceeding if you had executed a Durable Financial Power of Attorney and a healthcare power of attorney, giving someone else the authority to make these kinds of decisions for you.

Check out the statistics. People are living longer and longer. Their bodies may be fully functioning, but their brains are deteriorating. Alzheimer's and dementia are practically guaranteed if you live long enough. Planning for mental disability is just as important as planning for death.

4 **Create your plan without the help of a professional.**
Estate planning is not a DIY project. There are just too many ways to f$$k it up. When doing your estate plan, choose a lawyer specializing in estate planning and/or elder law. Better yet, get someone who is credentialed with a board certification or specialty designation in the area of practice. Only committed lawyers take the time and invest the effort to get these credentials.

Competent estate planning requires an extraordinary amount of knowledge and expertise. Not only do you have to know something about just about every other kind of law, but you also have to be skilled in psychology, counseling, and family dynamics. Estate planning and elder law attorneys must understand contract law, real estate law, probate law, trust law, tax law, family law, pet law, and guardianship law, just to name a few. If you haven't been to law school, then you probably don't know enough about any one of these subjects to anticipate even a few of the things that could go wrong with an improperly crafted estate plan. A qualified professional will be skilled in teaching you the questions you didn't know to ask and possessing the ability to convey complex ideas to you in simple-to-understand English.

5 Execute your plan improperly.
Do you know the execution requirements in your state to ensure your estate plan is executed properly? If the answer is yes, good for you. Refer to number 4 above. If the answer is no, then creating your own plan with the idea that you'll execute it properly is just wishful thinking.

Most states will require that your plan be signed by the creator and dated. That's just for starters. You may need two or more witnesses. These people should not be related to you, and they should not be beneficiaries of your estate. They all need to be present at the same time, in the same room, and in your presence, at the time you sign your Last Will, and they sign as your witnesses. Believe me; there is lots of litigation on this subject. You may need a notary. That notary may not also be one of the witnesses. The notary can't be related to you. You, your witnesses, and your notary all need to be in the same room, at the same time, when you sign your Last Will. Requirements vary from state to state, so be sure you know what your state law requires.

A Last Will or Trust that is improperly executed is the same as not having a plan. The default is your state's intestacy statutes.

6 **Work with the wrong professional.**
Most lawyers are not qualified to create a comprehensive estate plan that considers the big picture and meets their clients' goals. In fact, most lawyers, like most people, haven't even done their own estate plan. How can they be qualified to create yours?

If you have a friend, or a friend of a friend, who is a lawyer who will create your estate plan as a favor, thank them kindly and send them on their way. No good deed goes unpunished, and estate planning by unqualified attorney friends falls into this category. This would be analogous to hiring a doctor friend who is a gynecologist to perform your heart surgery. They simply aren't qualified to do the job right. And, since you don't know what you don't know, you don't know they haven't done it right. And, you won't be here (either mentally or physically) to find out. It will be your loved ones that suffer for your folly.

7 **Take advice from the wrong professionals - barbers, bankers, gardeners, plumbers, etc.**
My husband is a plumber. It's a worthy profession. However, I have heard him on the phone talking to friends, and he's giving legal advice! Really! I call this "the law according to Joe." I don't give plumbing advice; he shouldn't be giving legal advice. Well-meaning people can give you really bad advice.

I had a cleaning lady try to give me tax advice. Bankers fall into the category of professionals who give some of the worst estate planning advice. Their standard solution to any problem is to put another person's name on your account. It could be a family member or a friend. It doesn't matter what the person's relationship is to you. What they fail to understand, don't care to understand, and never explain is that the act of putting another person's name on your account makes that person an owner. Yep. Now your money is their money too. They can take that money out without your permission. Their creditors can have access to that money in the event of a catastrophic financial event. Their soon-to-be former spouse can claim an ownership interest in that money. You can die, and now it's all *their* money. And, consistent with what I said above, the new owner won't share their newfound wealth with your family or anyone you intended to also benefit from that money. Once the money is theirs and theirs alone, they will be singing a different tune.

Family members and friends give really bad advice too. Perhaps they heard a story about a friend who had an experience, blah blah blah. You've heard the stories. But they are likely only telling a portion of the story. They don't even know the back story. They probably don't have any of the facts of the situation correct. The information is second, third, or even fourth hand. Have you ever played the game called "operator" where the first person tells a story to the second person who tells it to the third and so on? The story at the end of the line isn't even remotely close to the original story. And, if the story took place in another state with different laws from the state you live in, well, you get the picture. The advice is not only wrong; it stinks and will most certainly not produce the desired result.

8 Ignore the advice of your professional advisors.
Everyone needs a team of professional advisors. You need a financial advisor. You need a tax advisor. You need an insurance

advisor. You need a legal advisor. You need a mental health advisor. You may even need a fashion advisor. We all need lots of advisors. But beware. This falls into the category of asking ten lawyers, doctors, bankers, electricians, plumbers, etc., a question, and you'll get 15 different answers! It's because there is no one-size-fits-all type of advice. All advice *depends*. It depends on your individual set of circumstances after all of the relevant facts have been examined. This is why advice solicited at cocktail parties always turns out to be bad advice. The giver of the advice never has enough information to give the proper guidance.

9 Not understanding what your plan says.

Maybe you created an estate plan. I'm impressed. Now explain it to me. If you're like most folks, you have absolutely no idea what your estate plan says. You knew or thought you knew what it said at the time it was created. But time has a way of marching on, and since then, you've crammed lots of new information into your head.

Or, you may have never known what your plan said, and you didn't care to learn. Estate plans are complex. There are lots of different legal documents. There are lots of moving parts. You likely did not go to law school, so some of the terms, strategies, techniques, etc., are new and unfamiliar to you. That's okay, but you should at least have a fundamental understanding of what happens in the event you become disabled and in the event of your death.

When I met one of my clients, he told me he didn't need my services because he had an estate plan. I congratulated him. Good job. Then, he asked me if I would explain his plan to him. He had absolutely no idea what his plan said; he couldn't even remember

7

what it was intended to accomplish. When I reviewed and then explained it to him, it bore no resemblance to what he wanted or what he thought he had. Lesson learned. We created a new estate plan that accomplished his estate planning goals.

10 Fail to review and update your plan periodically.

Estate planning is never a one-and-done project. Unless, of course, you can tell me exactly when you will die or become incapacitated, and we do your plan the day before. The fact of the matter is "s$$t happens," and "life happens fast." Both of these laws of nature will impact your estate plan. So will changes in the law of your state and the federal government, changes in your life including your financial situation, changes in the experience of your professional advisors, and changes in your legacy -- who you want to benefit from your estate plan and how you want them to benefit.

My husband once said to his son, Cody, "Be careful; one day, you are going to wake up from a nap and realize you are thirty." On the day he turned thirty, Cody called his dad and exclaimed, "OMG! I just woke up from a nap, and look what happened; now I'm thirty!" It happens to all of us. Our life is flashing before our eyes at warp speed. It feels impossible to get everything done in a day that needs to be done. People in retirement regularly report they don't know how they ever had time to work; they are just too busy.

Most Americans have never done an estate plan. Those who have probably haven't looked at them in more than a decade. The National Network of Estate Planning Attorneys once did an informal survey and discovered that the national average for updating an estate plan is 19.6 years! Has anything happened in the last 20 years of your life that has impacted your estate plan?

Do you think the laws have changed during that period? Has your attorney gotten any more intelligent? Are they still living and practicing? Do you still want to provide for the people and pets you love in the same way you did 20 years ago? Your kids have likely grown up, you may have grandkids, and the dog you had 20 years ago isn't the same one you have today. Heck, you might not even be married to the same person.

Your life can change in so many ways. You may have more money. You may have less money. Your health might be better than it was, but more likely, it's worse. Your family has certainly matured and changed. Your friends may have moved on, either literally or figuratively.

Your attorney's experience has changed too. If you hired me to prepare your estate plan 20 years ago, I did the very best job I could do for you at that time with the knowledge and experience I had. Today, I could likely do a much better job because I've had that much more experience with life, people, bad things that happen to good people, etc.

The law changes constantly. Otherwise, what are we paying all those politicians for? Every time there is a new administration or a new governor, the laws change. Judges change laws every day with their decisions. Bad facts make bad laws. How can you stay abreast of all the changes in the law? It's impossible. No one can do it. Even the pros have a hard time staying on top of all the laws and their changing nature. Even a small change in a law can have a significant impact on your estate plan.

How about changes in your legacy - the "who and the how" you want to leave your estate? Has that changed in recent years? I'm willing to bet it has.

Our firm offers a formal updating, education, and maintenance program, one of the few in the United States, and we meet with our clients periodically to review their estate plans. I'm always amazed at how frequently the who and the how change. I update my own estate plan regularly, and I'm constantly changing the who and the how. I'm sure I'm not unique. I've reviewed estate plans that were so old that the who and the how in their existing plan would have resulted in a complete failure of their estate plan to provide for the people they love.

How do you communicate changes in your life or your legacy to your professional advisors? Do you call them every time you have a life change? Do you meet with them periodically throughout the years? It's hard enough to get people to go to their doctor for an annual physical. Most only meet with their financial advisor and accountant once a year, if that often. I'm guessing your estate planning attorney isn't high on your list of people you want to spend time with (unless, of course, it's me), especially if they send you a bill to go with that visit. Make a point to review your estate plan each year when you do your taxes. If you have changes, don't wait. Call your attorney and update your estate plan today.

11 Fail to educate your family and friends about the role they have in your plan.

Let's assume you've worked with a professional, you've created an estate plan that you are happy with and that provides for your loved ones, that it is properly executed, and all of your assets are owned consistent with your intentions. Great job.

Now, all you've got to do is communicate this information to the people you have named in key roles so: 1. They are aware they have a future job ahead of themselves, and they are on board for this task; 2. They know where they can locate your plan and all of the supporting financial information; and 3. They know who your advisors are so that they can reach out for assistance at the appropriate time.

I'm stunned when I speak to family members who relate that their parent, friend, or loved one never mentioned they had a key role in their estate plan and never provided them with the basic information they would need to help carry out the plan in an efficient and low-stress manner.

When people die, families go on "a morbid scavenger hunt." They have to turn houses upside down, searching for pertinent legal and financial documents. It's worse now since much of our life is online, and our nominated helpers may not have any clue how to access that part of our life. Make sure you maintain a list of passwords and other information necessary to access your online life. Many states and many online organizations now offer the ability to name a "digital assets representative" to access this information legally. Your digital life can include everything from your phone to your computer to your social media accounts to your online access to your financial institutions.

If your plan can't be located, it may be determined you didn't have a plan. If you took the time to make one, take the time to make sure someone knows where to find it. Introduce your family to your attorney so they feel comfortable when the time comes to work with that individual or firm.

12 Select the wrong individuals to carry out your estate plan.

The persons you select to carry out your estate plan can include your Executor (Personal Representative), Successor Trustee, Agent under a Financial Power of Attorney, Agent/Surrogate under a

Healthcare Power of Attorney or Living Will, or other legal designees. The people you choose can actually make or break your plan. You should select only those individuals you would trust with your checkbook, who you know are reliable and detail-oriented, and who will carry out a job to its completion. Don't select someone because they are related to you or because they are your oldest son, the oldest child, or some other criteria that have nothing to do with the actual responsibilities they will be required to carry out.

Estate administration gets a bad name for many reasons, some of which can be blamed on the delays of the system or the law firm you've selected as your advisor. However, most of the time, the delays, the causes of litigation, and the waste in an estate are directly related to the capabilities of the person you've selected to carry out your wishes.

When family members fail to carry out their duties diligently and adequately, it is not uncommon for a lawsuit to ensue among family members. Litigation attorneys are the only ones that win in this scenario. They may view the value of your estate as the "war chest" they can access for their fees while simultaneously destroying any hope of reconciliation or family harmony for the future. And, when the money's gone, all that's left is the family's misery.

13 Fail to understand how asset ownership and beneficiary designations affect your plan.

This is one of the top three reasons estate plans fail. There is a widely held belief that your Last Will is the last word on how your estate will be distributed, regardless of how you own your assets or who you've named as your pay-on-death beneficiaries. Nothing could be further from the truth.

In reality, your Last Will only controls those assets you own in your individual name and on which you have not named a pay-on-death beneficiary. I'll say it again; your Last Will ONLY controls those assets you own in your individual name and on which you have not named a pay-on-death beneficiary. If you have taken the advice of your banker, financial advisor, or best friend and have added another person's name to your account because it was "convenient," you must understand that person now owns the account. Your Last Will is IRRELEVANT to who owns your account when you die. Similarly, if you have named only one of your children as the pay-on-death beneficiary of your retirement plan because you believe that child "will do the right thing and share with his siblings," I have news for you: they won't, and they don't. Your named beneficiary is the rightful owner of that asset at the time of your death. Your Last Will is IRRELEVANT.

If you name your best friend as the beneficiary of your life insurance and then you are no longer best friends, tough luck for your family while your former friend laughs all the way to the bank. In some states, if your now former spouse is named as a beneficiary of your retirement plan or life insurance, then sorry for the bad luck of your current spouse and your children. Some states have changed their laws to avoid this troublesome outcome.

Without a beneficiary designation on life insurance, retirement plans, or other contracts that allow such a designation, that asset will likely end up as part of your probate estate.

You may have created a living trust and included provisions to ensure the money you leave to your loved ones is protected when they receive it. You can craft a trust to protect the people you love from the bad things that happen to good people (like a divorce or a catastrophic creditor event); to protect them from themselves if they have a spending, gambling, drug, or alcohol problem; and protect and preserve their government benefits if they have a disability. Suppose you've incorporated these types of protections into your Living Trust. In that case, you'll absolutely want to make sure your beneficiary designations don't cause that money to accidentally bypass the trust instructions you've intentionally created for your loved ones' benefit.

Suppose you designate a minor child, an incompetent person, or a person who needs to be protected from himself (could be for any number of reasons mentioned above) as a pay-on-death beneficiary. In that case, you have f$$k'd up your plan because that person is now the legal owner of that asset. Don't let that happen.

14 Move to another state and never update your plan.
Estate plans are portable and in accordance with the full faith and credit provisions of our United States Constitution, a plan created in one state should be valid in another. However, laws vary widely from state to state. If you move to another state and plan to stay there, the next time you update your estate plan, you should consider getting a qualified professional in that state who can ensure your plan will work within your new state's laws.

15 Fail to understand the basics of probate.
Probate is not a four-letter word. It is not the state "taking your money." It IS a state governed process for the purpose of "proving your will" or distributing your estate to your intestate heirs in the absence of a Last Will.

Every state has its own rules about how this process is accomplished. Some states have multiple processes depending on the value of your estate. Some of these processes are shorter than others. Most will require hiring an attorney, paying attorney fees and costs, and following the rules of the state where you lived at the time of your death.

One of the pros and also one of the cons of probate is it is a court-administered process. This means a judge oversees the process to make sure things run smoothly, everybody is honest, and the right people get your estate. The fact it is a court-administered process is also its con - it means there will likely be a cost involved (court fees and attorney fees) and will require an investment of time. It will also be a public process that does not guarantee privacy.

Probate essentially consists of three (3) steps:

(1) **Identify and gather the assets of the estate.** These are the assets that are owned in the INDIVIDUAL name of the deceased. These assets will also include checks made payable to the deceased after death when car insurance, health insurance, and homeowner's insurance are canceled, and the unearned premium is refunded. It also includes any income tax refunds due to the deceased after filing final tax returns.

(2) **Identify and pay the creditors of the estate.** Every state will have its own process to accomplish this task. Generally, it requires giving notice to known creditors (those that are sending bills to the home of the deceased) and publishing in a widely-circulated notice to unknown creditors (those that may be waiting in the wings for the debtor to die). In some states, this also requires giving notice to Medicare, Medicaid, and the state Department of Revenue to be notified if they have any claims. There is generally no requirement to notify the Internal Revenue Service (IRS) because they are a super creditor and always have the right to be paid first.

Then there will be a specified period of time when creditors have the right to come forward and file their claims against the estate. I usually refer to this period as "speak now or forever hold your peace," just like they say in some weddings. If a creditor fails to file their claim on time, the claim will be barred. If they timely file a claim and it is a legitimate claim, the creditor has a right to be paid. If the creditor files a claim and it is not a legitimate claim, the Personal Representative will have the right to object to the claim. Once a claim is objected to, the creditor has an obligation to file a lawsuit to enforce the claim, or it is considered abandoned. At the end of the creditor claim period, state statutes "rank" the claims according to their priority after identifying legitimate claims.

The IRS always gets paid first. So do the attorneys, accountants, and others who have participated in the administration process. Funeral homes and medical providers at the end of life may also have a priority claim. Secured creditors have the asset that has been pledged (a home, car, boat, etc.) as the primary source of their payment but may also file a claim for any deficiency. Lesser claims like credit cards and unsecured creditors are generally paid last. If the estate assets are insufficient to pay all of the claims, some creditors (and unfortunately, now the beneficiaries) will not receive payment.

Some creditors may be willing to compromise their claims and take a smaller payment in exchange for not getting paid at all. Some estate assets will be "exempt from the claims of creditors" and won't be available to pay creditor claims.

(3) **Distribute the assets that are left to the rightful heirs or named beneficiaries.** It seems like this should be the easiest part of the estate administration process, but that isn't always the case. Sometimes identifying the rightful heirs can be a problem. This

is especially true if the deceased has been married multiple times and has a trail of kids all around the country or the world. It can be further complicated if the deceased adopted any children or allowed any of their children to be adopted by someone else.

I have a case right now where the husband died without a will. He was married to his third wife. He had two biological children with his first wife. They also adopted a child, making three. Later, he had two biological children with his second wife. He allowed these two children to be adopted by another man after the dissolution of that marriage. He had no children with his third wife. He never made a Last Will, and I now have some very interesting conversations with his family.

In another case, my client discovered he had a biological daughter he wasn't aware of until she was in her sixties. When he was a young man, he visited Daytona Beach on Spring Break and met a girl. You know the rest of the story; only he was never made aware that he had a child. Today's technology allows us to identify persons who share our DNA and are likely related to us. It was this technology that introduced father and daughter. This story seems like it should have a happy ending, but my client is still alive, and his two younger daughters are less than thrilled that they have to share their future inheritance with their new sister. He is currently in a lawsuit defending his honor and his right to benefit all of his children. Seriously, you can't make this s$$t up, and it happens all the time.

Sometimes the named beneficiaries have predeceased the newly deceased, and there may need to be a determination of their legal successor. Sometimes a beneficiary dies after the newly deceased but before the assets have been distributed. Now there has to be an administration of that individual's estate and a determination of their rightful heirs. If the beneficiary is a minor, an incompetent, or has creditor claims of their own, then there may be additional complications, delays, and expenses.

Estate administration should be simple, but it rarely is.

16 Fail to understand trust administration is a process too.

One of the benefits of a Revocable Living Trust (RLT) is that it can avoid probate. However, a trust does not avoid administration. There is still stuff to do when the grantor (Trustmaker) of a trust dies, and it looks a lot like probate administration without the supervision of the court.

Like a court-administered probate, the privacy associated with a trust administration can be both a pro and a con. The pro is there is no court involved, no court filing fees, no judge looking over the shoulder of your Successor Trustee. Lack of supervision can also be a big con. Since there is no court process, many Successor Trustees assume they do not need to hire a lawyer to guide them through the process.

No court supervision, lots of privacy. In private, people do things they wouldn't do in a public arena. Pick the wrong Successor Trustee, and your beneficiaries may never see a single dime.

Unsupervised Successor Trustees may be unaware of the laws governing the administration of trusts. They may fail to give notice to the court of the existence of the trust. They may fail to give notice and a copy of the trust to the named beneficiaries. They may fail to notify the creditors of the estate. They may fail to file required tax returns. They may fail to distribute the assets as required by the trust instrument. In other words, they may completely f**k up the administration of the trust. Family member beneficiaries may suspect they are getting the shaft but won't complain because they want to maintain family harmony. Or, family member beneficiaries may complain and then file a lawsuit against their sibling Successor Trustee. The litigators win - again!

It is not unusual for a trust to have language that provides for ongoing trusts after the initial administration at the death of the Trustmaker. These ongoing trusts could be a trust for the benefit of a surviving spouse to minimize future exposure to estate tax, to protect them in the event of remarriage, or to protect children from previous marriages.

Another purpose for an ongoing trust could be to benefit children with a lifetime protective trust to ensure creditor protection and divorce protection. Trusts can also protect children with spending, drug, alcohol, or gambling dependency disorders. Special needs trusts can be created for children with special needs to preserve eligibility for government benefits. Trusts can also be used for the benefit of other loved ones, including aging parents or pets.

Ongoing trusts require ongoing administration. They need to be properly established according to the requirements of the trust. Tax identification numbers need to be obtained, and trust tax returns (Form 1041) must be filed. Trustees need to be properly appointed, and Affidavits or Certificates of Trust need to be executed. Once the resulting trusts have been established, they require ongoing management. The Trustee has numerous fiduciary obligations regarding the investment, management, distribution, taxation, and reporting requirements of the trust assets.

Sometimes, Successor Trustees or well-meaning financial advisors simply distribute the trust's assets without regard for the trust's actual requirements. Not only is this a breach of the Trustees' fiduciary duty, but it can also be catastrophic for the beneficiaries.

17 Fail to understand the differences between a Last Will and a Revocable Living Trust.

Wills and trusts, including Revocable Living Trusts (RLT), have different purposes. Sometimes these purposes are complimentary, but they usually accomplish different goals. As mentioned, a Last Will is only relevant for assets that are owned in your individual name. A Last Will is only operative at the time of your death - it has no function during your lifetime.

An RLT is only relevant for assets: 1. re-titled to the name of the trust; 2. where the RLT is the named beneficiary; or 3. received as the "pour over" recipient from a Last Will. An RLT is designed to be effective during your lifetime, in the event of your disability, and at the time of your death.

A Last Will is not a trust, but a Last Will can have resulting testamentary trusts included in its language. A testamentary trust is a form of "standby" trust that exists only in theory until the death of the Testator (the person who wrote the Last Will). Likewise, an RLT that operates during your lifetime, in the event of your disability, and at your death may also have resulting testamentary trusts.

Confused? Don't be, but the point is this stuff is tough to understand, and there are lots of ways to f$$k it up.

18 Fail to create a strong disability plan including Financial Durable Power of Attorney, Healthcare Power of Attorney, and Living Will as part of your comprehensive estate plan.

Every comprehensive estate plan will include a "disability plan" that contemplates what happens in the event you become mentally incapacitated during your lifetime. Someday, we will all die.

Before that, many of us will experience a period of disability. This is a time during your life I refer to as "alive, but not well." You are still alive, but you cannot manage your financial affairs or make your own health care decisions due to a decline in your mental or physical capabilities.

The ability to make decisions on behalf of another is not automatic, despite your status as a spouse or parent. The written legal delegation of the right to make decisions on behalf of another is required. Generally, these legal instruments fall into the category of a Durable Financial Power of Attorney (DPOA), a Healthcare Power of Attorney (HCPOA), and Living Will or other advance directives.

The individuals named as your "helpers" in these instruments are supposed to do what you would do, under the circumstances. They should not be making decisions that benefit themselves or create conflicts of interest.

A comprehensive disability plan is intended to ensure you do not become the victim of a forced guardianship. A guardianship is the worst kind of lawsuit. It is one your family files against you; you get to pay for it, and then you lose. It is a complete loss of autonomy and the ability to make your own decisions. The best way to avoid guardianship is with proper legal directives.

A Durable Financial Power of Attorney is an absolute requirement if you want someone else to be able to manage your legal and financial affairs in the event of your disability. A Successor Trustee for a Revocable Living Trust has financial responsibilities regarding the assets held in the trust. However, the agent named in the DPOA may actually have a broader, more expansive role because they are responsible for all activities and assets outside of the RLT. State law may require the grant of powers to be absolutely specific to be valid. Elder law planning for long-term care asset protection also requires provisions that may not be available if you work with the wrong professional or try to do this yourself.

A HCPOA is the legal instrument that delegates your decision-making for everyday medical care decisions. These are decisions like consent to surgery, consent to treatment, transfer to and from a medical facility, and the hiring and firing of doctors, nurses, therapists, caregivers, etc. These nominated individuals may also have consent to access your medical records and speak with your medical professionals under HIPAA (Health Insurance Portability & Accountability Act).

A Living Will is your end-of-life expression regarding how you want to be cared for if you cannot express your desires. Typically, it authorizes the withdrawal or refusal to accept life-prolonging procedures such as artificial hydration, nutrition, and respiration. A Living Will may instruct that you be kept comfortable, provided with pain-relieving medications but ultimately, allowed to die without artificial interference. The opposite of a Living Will is what I call a Will to Live. This is a person's expression requesting (as opposed to refusing) life-prolonging procedures.

A Living Will is not a DNR (Do Not Resuscitate) directive. A DNR can only be obtained through and after consultation with your doctor. It is not a document drafted by your attorney.

19 Fail to understand that debts and taxes may have to be paid at death.

Ben Franklin said, "Nothing is certain in life but death and taxes." This is mostly true. We all will die; we just don't know when or how. And, we will have to pay our taxes; we just don't know how much.

The tax laws change on a very regular basis. Each time they do, my partner and I refer to the change as "The attorney and CPA job protection act." Taxes have gotten so complicated that keeping up with them can be a full-time job. This is a strong reason why everyone needs to have a team of trusted advisors, including a tax professional.

Death doesn't avoid the obligation to pay your debts or your taxes. There may be planning strategies that can help you eliminate or minimize taxes, but ultimately, you'll still be responsible for your tax debt without a plan. You may remember I said that the IRS is a super creditor. Still true.

There are lots of advanced planning strategies to minimize or eliminate estate taxes. Suppose your estate (that means everything you own, everything you control, and everything your name is on) is substantial or growing. In that case, you'll be best served by consulting with your professional advisor team to make sure you and your loved ones don't receive an unexpected and hefty income or estate tax bill.

20 Fail to understand the basics of gift taxes.

The gift tax system allows you to give money away during your lifetime to minimize or avoid the estate tax. You can make annual exclusion gifts, and you can use your lifetime estate tax exemption to make more significant gifts while you are alive.

Annual exclusion gifts can be made to as many people as you desire. These are gifts you don't have to report to the IRS. If you have a spouse, you can double your annual exemption using gift-splitting. Gifts to individuals can be made outright or in a trust. Gifts to a trust require you to give up sufficient control of the asset to avoid having it pulled back into your taxable estate at the time of death. This is a common way to screw up planning with irrevocable trusts. If the donor retains too much control and the IRS refuses to acknowledge the gift, the planning strategy has failed, resulting in significant tax.

Lifetime gifts that use up your lifetime estate tax exemption are another strategy for reducing your taxable estate and/or taking advantage of higher exemption amounts today that may be reduced in the future due to a change in the tax laws. There are also strategies to make gifts to your spouse that meet the requirement of giving up control while still allowing the donor to benefit from the assets.

If you make gifts directly to an educational institution or a medical facility, you may be able to make unlimited gifts that do not use any of your annual or lifetime exclusions. Gifts to charity are another way to reduce or eliminate your exposure to estate taxes. This way, you choose your philanthropy - the United States government by paying taxes or a charity of your choice by making strategic donations.

Advanced estate gift and estate tax planning is highly complex and is not for the uninitiated. There are too many ways to make too many mistakes. Those mistakes may not be discovered until after you die when it's too late to do anything but fight with the IRS and/or pay the tax.

21 Fail to understand the basics of estate taxes.

When you die, your nominated and appointed representative needs to file your final tax return. This can be easy or hard, depending on how organized you were during your lifetime. If your estate exceeds the estate tax exemption amount or you want to claim your spouse's unused estate tax exemption, then an estate tax Form 706 will be required.

The estate tax return is due nine (9) months after the date of death, with some opportunity to possibly extend. The tax, if any, is still due. The way to remember when the return is due is that it takes nine months to come into this world and nine months to pay your estate taxes on your way out!

As mentioned, there are lots of strategies to reduce or avoid gift and estate taxes. None are automatic, and most involve giving up control. Frequently they are complicated and require the ongoing attention of you and your trusted advisors. This falls into the category of there is no such thing as a free lunch. You may have to employ legal techniques that you wouldn't otherwise even consider to avoid estate taxes.

Everyone needs to understand the basics of estate taxes. There's just no excuse to leave an unexpected surprise to your family when you had the ability and the opportunity to address the situation when you were alive. Of course, you could fall into the category of persons who say, "I don't care what happens when I die." And, that is your prerogative. Just know, if that's true, you've likely left an estate planning disaster in your wake.

If your estate consists primarily of real estate or business interests and you have a taxable estate, then the property or the business will likely need to be sold to pay the taxes due. Life insurance or financial investments can help create liquidity for your estate so that hard to sell or hard to value assets can be retained by your loved ones. Creating a pot of money outside your taxable estate is another way to ease the liquidity requirements for tax payment at your death.

22 Fail to understand the basics of income taxes.

Income taxes are the contribution we make annually to our government for the opportunity to live in the United States. If you work or invest and earn an income, you'll likely be required to pay income taxes. They are due every year on April 15.

Included in income taxes are capital gains taxes. This is the tax you pay when you buy something at a low price and sell it at a high one. The price you pay is called your basis. The price you sell it for is the sales price, hopefully, fair market value. The difference is the profit on which you pay tax. If you hold the asset for less than a year, you'll have short-term gains. If you hold the asset for more than a year, you'll have long-term gains that enjoy a more favorable tax rate. This is the IRS incentive for longer-term investing versus day trading.

When you give an asset away during your lifetime, you give away the basis in that asset. If you paid $10 for a share of Coca-Cola and now it is worth $100 a share, your donee (the person you gave it to) receives the asset with your $10 per share basis. If they sell it for $100, they owe capital gains tax on the $90 per share profit. You gave them a nice gift, but you also gave them a capital gains tax. If you wait until your death to give away your assets, your loved ones inherit that asset at their date of death value (this can be lower, but hopefully higher than what you paid for it.) If your heir sells the property at the date of death value, there should be no exposure to capital gains. So, there is a benefit to holding on to some assets until the end of your life.

The capital gains tax is also subject to change. Stay abreast of these changes to ensure you aren't creating a tax bomb for your loved ones. Charities don't pay income tax, so making a gift of appreciated assets to charity is a good capital gains avoidance technique.

Some assets, like your primary residence, may enjoy preferential capital gains treatment during your lifetime. This allows you to sell your home and either downsize or upsize without paying capital gains tax.

Taxes are complex. Always consult with your tax professionals before making gifts or liquidating assets.

23 Neglect to save and plan for your future retirement.

No one can live on Social Security alone. Some would even argue that Social Security may not be around when you need it. And I would venture to guess you didn't work your whole life to end up homeless or relying on your friends and family for support.

Become a saver; it's a cultivated habit. There's an old investment adage, "Pay yourself first." This means to set aside a portion of each paycheck toward an emergency fund, then savings for your retirement. If you don't save, no one is going to do it for you. Start young and save often.

The power of compounding and investing for long-term results will help. The Rule of 72 is a mathematical formula to determine how fast your money will double. Divide the rate of return into 72 for the number of years it takes to double your money. For example, if you are earning a 10% rate of return, money doubles every 7.2 years. Likewise, a 2% rate of return requires 36 years before your money doubles. That's a huge difference. This formula does not account for taxes or a loss in purchasing power due to inflation. Choose tax-deferred investments for the best long-term results and the power of triple compounding.

Work with a qualified financial professional to teach you how to maximize your returns while minimizing your risk exposure. We each have a risk tolerance, and some investments won't be appealing because of their risk. Other investments that offer more security will have a lower rate of return. The higher the risk, the higher the possible reward.

Invest using a pyramid approach with the base of the pyramid representing your safest investments. This is where the bulk of your savings should be. As you move up the pyramid, you can increase your level of risk and potential reward. Never put all your eggs in one basket. If it's too good to be true, it probably is. There are no guaranteed investments. This is all good advice and not just platitudes that are fun to share.

24 Wait too long to plan.

I've talked about the importance of planning for mental disability. Many will not take this advice and wait until there is a crisis before deciding it is finally time to act. Wait too long, and you may be f$$ked. If you do not have the mental competence to sign your legal estate planning documents, then the only other option will be a forced guardianship - the dreaded lawsuit brought by your family against you, but ultimately for the purpose of protecting you.

Mental incapacity is also one of the reasons family members challenge planning. If a person is believed not to have the mental capacity to execute a Durable Financial Power of Attorney, Last Will or Living Trust, disgruntled family members may challenge the planning. The family members most likely to institute this type of challenge generally are not the friendliest ones. Or, they may be trying to right a wrong perpetrated by another unscrupulous family member.

In any event, a person is required to have the mental capacity to sign legal documents. The capacity standard can vary based on the type of document being signed. Without proper capacity, the planning may be determined invalid and worthless.

If you don't have a plan, your state has one for you. Your state will provide the rules for guardianship in the event of mental disability and rules for the distribution of your estate when you die without a Last Will or Living Trust.

25 Leave the door open for family conflict - only the lawyers win.

When families fight, only lawyers win. That's as blunt as I can be. Lawsuits are expensive, they take a long time, and they are emotionally and physically draining. A family lawsuit generally doesn't result in family harmony. There isn't a big, joyful family re-union when it's over. More likely, the family unit will be destroyed, and family members will be estranged. Forever.

In my own family, my grandfather worked in the family busi-ness. He always believed when his father died; he would inherit the business. That was what he was told. However, when his dad died, his mother decided to give the business to the three sons equally, two of whom never worked in the business. My grandfather never spoke to his brothers again. If my great grandfather wanted his son, who devoted his life to the business, to inherit the business, he should have taken the proper legal steps to ensure this result. Instead, he relied on his spouse to carry out this goal.

One thing is certain. Kids all want to be treated equally. It doesn't matter if one of them has the wealth of Bill Gates. However, parents often believe they need to give more to the child or chil-dren who "need the most help." This is a recipe for disaster. I've interviewed hundreds of families, and the kids all say the same thing - they just want to be treated equally.

Likely, the children were not equal when they were growing up. The ones who were more capable sometimes got less, while those that were needier got more. Siblings are competitive by nature. In their minds, equal is fair. Sometimes it is, sometimes it isn't. It doesn't matter. If you don't plan to treat your children equally, plan on a future fight.

There are right ways and wrong ways to disinherit people if you really want to. Your trusted legal advisors can provide you with advice that is appropriate for your family and your goals.

26 Fail to specify the distribution of sentimental or valuable personal property.

Families love to fight over stuff. Your stuff is your personal property. It includes your jewelry, furniture, fixtures, collectibles, automobiles, etc. It is the stuff we buy bigger houses for because we get too much stuff. Your personal property often doesn't have much actual value, but it can have a lot of sentimental value.

Families fight over all kinds of stuff; Beanie Baby collections, Pez dispenser collections, a sword awarded to a marine service member, mom's engagement ring, etc. You name it; if it has sentimental or perceived actual value, families will fight over it.

Most of our stuff is junk. But we don't view it that way, and some of our family members don't either. We think stuff is valuable. Value is only in the eye of the beholder. Most of our stuff is actually worthless - meaning, what someone else is willing to pay for it.

My sister owns an antique store. Everything our parents thought was valuable is available for sale in her store. No one is buying any of it. I have a friend who has an estate liquidation business. She has this business because no one wants the stuff in your estate. **It sells at liquidation value. Stuff you think is valuable probably isn't.**

If your family fights over your stuff, it is only valuable to the lawyers and what they can charge to settle the dispute between your family members. Sometimes estate settlement is like a divorce. We fight over the dumbest things; beach chairs, Tervis tumblers, stamp or coin collections, etc.

Do yourself a favor. If you think you have valuable stuff, sell it during your lifetime so you can supervise the sale and make sure it ends up in a good home. If you don't oversee the sale of your stuff, your kids will offer it for sale to the highest bidder, if any. If they think it's worthless, it will end up at Goodwill - but only if they take it. Otherwise, it will end up in the trash.

Our great grandmother's Minton china ended up at Goodwill because no one in our family wanted it. No one uses fine china anymore. My estate liquidation friend tells me her biggest buyer of fine china these days is shooting ranges - process that. Stuff you think is valuable is someone else's target practice.

Do yourself a favor, write down who gets what. Give it away or sell it during your lifetime. That way, there won't be any fights, and the person you left it to won't have the problem of getting rid of it.

27 Get a divorce and fail to update your planning, asset ownership, and beneficiary designations.

A divorce is a major life-changing event. You are no longer married. You are now a single person. Now is the time to update your estate planning, review your asset ownership and update your beneficiary designations. No one is going to do it for you.

If you don't do it and you die or become disabled, your family may discover they have a big surprise in store. Depending on state law, your former spouse may still be the legal beneficiary on assets like retirement plans and life insurance. In other states, the act of getting divorced severs all beneficiary designations. That would be the good news. However, without a proper beneficiary, your estate will be your default beneficiary with all of the problems associated with that default option.

If your divorce changed your relationship with your children, you'd want to consider that consequence too. Bottom line; If you get a divorce, update your estate planning and your beneficiary designations.

28 Leave assets to non-U.S. Citizens.

The estate and gift tax laws that apply to non-U.S. Citizens are not the same as U.S. Citizens. If you are married to a non-citizen spouse, it is important to know this.

You do not have the advantage of the "unlimited marital deduction," meaning you can give your U.S. spouse an unlimited amount of assets without having to report the gift to the IRS. You also are limited on the annual gifts you can give a non-U.S. citizen spouse without having to report the gift to the IRS.

And there are special rules for leaving assets at your death to non-U.S. citizen spouses. There is an assumption when you leave money to non-U.S. citizens; they will take the money and leave the country. So there are taxes and restrictions that apply. In some cases, you'll need to create a Qualified Domestic Order Trust (QDOT) to successfully leave assets to a non-U.S citizen spouse.

29 Fail to elect portability at the death of a spouse.

Portability, also known as Deceased Spouse Unused Exemption (DSUE), is the ability of a surviving spouse to claim the unused estate tax exemption of the first spouse to die. For example, if your spouse dies and leaves all of their assets to you, the surviving spouse, then they haven't used any of their lifetime estate tax exemption. Instead, they used their unlimited marital deduction.

Of course, if they used up some or all of their lifetime exemption during their lifetime, those lifetime gifts will be deducted from the lifetime exemption amount. When there is unused exemption, the surviving spouse can file a Form 706 Estate Tax Return and claim the unused exemption. In some cases, this will allow the surviving spouse to double their estate tax exemption amount. At a time when the estate tax exemption may be lowered, this can be an advantage to the surviving spouse. They will have the DSUE amount, and they will have their own exemption at the time of their death.

To claim the unused exemption of a deceased spouse, the Form 706 must be filed timely. If you miss the filing date, you will forfeit the portability of the exemption.

Some people will assume they will never have enough assets to worry about spousal portability. That's your gamble. Maybe you will; maybe you won't. Why not be safe rather than sorry? All it costs is some time, energy, and the price of a tax return. Consult with your professional advisor team for their opinion.

30 Neglect to administer a joint trust at the death of the first spouse.

Couples have been planning with joint trusts for decades. The problem is there is a general assumption there is nothing to do at the first spouse's death. Read those trusts, and another answer appears.

The trust may say that a portion of the trust becomes irrevocable when the first spouse dies, and a portion remains revocable. There may even be estate tax planning in the trust that could result in the creation of two irrevocable trusts - one that captures the estate tax exemption (credit shelter) of the first to die and one that uses the unlimited marital deduction (marital trust).

If a joint trust is not properly administered at the first spouse's death, then trying to administer it years later is messy business. It may actually require forensic accounting. You can bet that won't be cheap.

This is one of the problems with joint trusts. A surviving spouse and their advisors are often unaware of what is required when the first spouse dies. If not properly administered, many of the benefits of the planning may be lost. As a general rule, our office never recommended joint trust planning for couples until DSUE was enacted, allowing the surviving spouse to claim the unused exemption of the first to die. And even now, we recommend keeping the joint trust fully revocable and amendable on the first spouse's death. That way, when the first spouse dies, there truly is no administration required, and the surviving spouse still can amend and revoke the trust.

If this is your second or more marriage, a joint trust that remains revocable at your death may not be a good idea. You may not want to leave everything to your current spouse and under their control. Instead, you may also want to plan to leave assets for the benefit of your children from previous relationships. The solution for you may be separate trusts - one for you and one for your spouse. Talk to your professional advisor team before you decide.

31 Forget about assets you own - unclaimed property.

It seems unlikely you would forget about the assets or money you have at a financial institution, but it happens all the time. SmartAsset currently reports there is something north of 49 billion dollars (that's with a "b") in unclaimed funds. Approximately 4 billion dollars are returned to their rightful owners annually. The National Association of Unclaimed Property Administrations estimates 1 in 10 people has unclaimed property. You can find more information at Unclaimed.org. Check this site annually when you review your taxes.

Unclaimed property is not an isolated event. It happens all the time. You create a small account, then move and forget you have it. Or a loved one created an account for you, and you lost track of it.

Most states have an unclaimed funds department. You should check online resources regularly to ensure you don't have money floating around you didn't know about. Beware of scams and never pay anyone to find "unclaimed funds" for you until you are sure they are a legitimate organization. One of my clients was contacted by an "heir search" company indicating there were assets to be inherited and all they had to do was pay a fee. Well, all they really had to do was call the attorney handling the estate and receive their inheritance. A simple search of the public records of the county where their aunt died revealed this information.

32 Keep secrets from your family - fail to share the big picture of your estate plan.

It's nice to have privacy, but you can share the overall goal of your estate plan with your loved ones without having to reveal all the details. Most importantly, your named "helpers" need to know where to find your important legal documents, who your team of trusted advisors is and how to locate your assets.

When buying real estate, the important thing is location, location, location. When settling an estate, the important thing is organization, organization, organization. If you are an unorganized person who keeps poor or non-existent records, then you can expect your loved ones will have a difficult, if not miserable, time trying to settle your estate.

One family brought me an office full of brown grocery bags containing hundreds of pieces of unopened mail, uncashed checks, requests for information, monthly statements, etc. It took a long time to sort through all the information and notify all of the relevant parties. Years later, the family was still finding unclaimed property, and more than once, we had to re-open the estate to probate newly discovered assets.

Searching for information after you die is called the morbid scavenger hunt. Death and its corresponding grief are tough enough without the aggravation of initiating a full-out search to discover assets. Do yourself and your loved ones a favor - create a notebook with relevant information and update it once a year. Your family will thank you. So will their attorney.

33 Be overly rigid in the design of your bequests.
This means trying to control too many outcomes or decisions from the grave. If you are going to create an estate plan, you have the right to impose any kind of restrictions you want - right? Sure, if you want to create ongoing stress for your loved ones.

What are you trying to control? Some restrictions are appropriate - especially those that provide the financially unsophisticated with protection from themselves, protection from drug, alcohol, or gambling disorders, divorce protection, bloodline protection, and creditor protection, just to name a few.

I'm thinking of an example where the deceased would only provide money for a college education if the recipient went to a specific school, his alma mater. That's his prerogative, but what if his kids/grandkids didn't have the aptitude to get into his alma mater? What if this person was unusually skilled as an artist or musician, and the best post-high school education for this person would be another institution of higher learning?

Another example is an individual could benefit from his aunt's estate during his lifetime, and his biological children could benefit after his lifetime. Unfortunately, he never had any biological children. However, he was married to a wonderful woman who had two lovely children. Despite the fact he adopted them, and they were his children for all other legal purposes, they were not his biological children, and he could not meet the definition under the trust. They were unable to benefit from his aunt's planning.

I also remember a situation where adopted children were included but only if they were adopted before the age of five (5). Sadly, several of the children were adopted after the age of five (5) but before they were ten (10). Too bad; they didn't meet the definition.

Then there are the restrictions that are actually illegal or against public policy. This type of restriction may attempt to prevent a family member from marrying someone outside their race, religion, or gender. This type of restriction cannot be legally enforced.

There's an old estate planning joke about a gentleman whose wife hated his cigar smoking. As a condition to receiving distributions from his trust, she was required to smoke a cigar!

Restrictions can range from the odd to the absurd. Consider the woman who left her brother "a rope to hang himself with." Or the man who was convinced he would return from the dead, so he left money for the preparation of a daily meal so he would have something to eat when he returned.

Truth is stranger than fiction.

34 Change your plan continuously in unpredictable ways or every time you get mad at someone.

Many movies and books have plots of revenge or disinheriting loved ones because of an argument or long-standing disagreement. People generally leave their estates to those persons they are closest to at the end of their lives. This may be their children, or it could be a close friend or neighbor. It may be a caregiver.

Your Last Will and Living Trust can be changed anytime you want, for any reason, provided you have the mental capacity to do so. We have clients that quite regularly change their final wishes depending on the quality of their relationship with certain key persons in their life at that time.

Know that if you make a change out of anger, and then you resolve the dispute but fail to update your estate plan, whatever is written in the last version of your estate plan is the one that prevails.

Changing your plan based on emotions can have negative outcomes if you happen to die while the most recent angry version of your plan exists. I don't recommend using your estate plan as a weapon with the threat of, "If you don't do so and so, I'm taking you out of my Will!"

35 Send mixed signals - or share your plan with the wrong people.

It isn't unusual for people to share parts of their plan or thoughts about their estate plan with the people they intend to provide for. However, creating an expectation of inheritance may send the wrong signal. If you change your mind later and decide not to provide for that person, you may have just purchased a lawsuit for your loved ones.

I had a client whose husband promised all his grandchildren he would leave them $100,000. Guess what? He didn't. He did, however, leave his surviving spouse a lawsuit from one of the grandsons who was intent on making that promise come true. And, despite the fact the grandson wasn't mentioned in the grandfather's estate plan, he found an attorney to take his case. The surviving spouse was forced to defend the lawsuit, and after more than $40,000 in attorneys' fees, they entered into a settlement agreement of an undisclosed amount - likely something at or near $100,000.

Theoretically, you should not be able to sue someone based on an inheritance expectancy. However, you can sue someone for just about anything, and you can likely find an attorney willing to take your case!

36 Let taxes drive your decisions.

Minimizing or eliminating estate taxes are good reasons to do an estate plan. However, letting the "tax tail" wag the "estate planning dog" can have disastrous results. Tax motivated planning can be very complex and requires ongoing maintenance and attention to ensure the plan's details remain consistent with your estate planning goals, the law, and your attorney's experience.

When taxes are the primary motivator for a plan, loved ones may pay the ultimate price - a loss of their inheritance to unexpected results, a lawsuit with the IRS, or a tax bill they can't pay.

37 Fail to consider how estate taxes may affect your plan and your loved ones.

Despite your best efforts, your estate may be subject to estate tax at the time of your death. If you have not considered how those taxes will affect your loved ones, there could be unexpected consequences. Estate taxes are due nine (9) months after the date of death. If your estate consists primarily of real property, illiquid investments (such as limited partnerships), or closely-held business interests, finding the cash to pay the IRS can be a challenge.

This is where the concept of a "fire sale" likely originated. A fire sale occurs when families are forced to sell assets at a discounted rate to raise capital to pay the IRS.

38 Fail to keep good records or any.

What kind of record keeper are you? Do you open your monthly statements, pay your bills, and then toss them in the trash? Do you save paid statements in a folder to be added to a box for use at the end of the year when you file your tax return? Do you do all of your financial transactions online and consider yourself to be paperless? Do you move frequently and lose important documents every time you make a move?

When my dad died, he had more than 125 notebooks full of financial information. Most of it was worthless as it was outdated and of little value to the relevant time period. He went to the other extreme. We had to hire a shredding company to come to the house as it would have been irresponsible to put that much financial information in the trash. Then we had the issue of disposing of the notebooks! Fortunately, we were able to deliver them to a local school for reuse.

One of my clients did all of his financial transactions online. When he died, no one knew how to access his computer or any of his online accounts. We had to hire a "professional hacker" to break into his computer to get the information necessary to settle his estate.

In the old days, when all bills arrived monthly in the U.S. mail, identifying assets and creditors was a lot easier. Today, much of our life is online, and accessing information can be a real challenge. If you use a password manager to keep up with your passwords, write down the master password and keep it with your important estate planning documents. Put it in a sealed envelope only to be opened in the event of your death. It is unlikely that a family member or loved one will know where you keep your password information. You should also keep your safe deposit box key with your important estate planning documents. Otherwise, the services of a locksmith and a court order to access your box will be required.

39 Trust someone to "do the right thing."

Wishful thinking isn't a plan. Hope is not a plan. Trusting someone to do the right thing isn't a plan either. It is simply a wish, one that will likely backfire. I can't count the number of times clients have told me their family knows what they want and will do the right thing. Baloney and bulls$$t! I can't count the number of times when these same trusted persons simply said, "Hell no."

One of the saddest cases I remember was when a young man was killed in a tragic accident. He had an infant son with a woman he wasn't married to. He worked for a good company that provided him with a substantial life insurance policy. He named his mother as the beneficiary because he was sure she would "do the right thing" and take care of his child and the child's mother. You can guess the outcome. The mother of the deceased simply took the money and continued to live her life without any concerns about the welfare of her grandchild.

This same story applies to putting one child's name on an asset or as a beneficiary on a retirement plan or life insurance policy, hoping they will share with their siblings. Ain't going to happen. They rarely, if ever, share.

It has been said, "People change when people die." Nothing could be more accurate. Money does change people. Sibling rivalries rear their ugly heads when a parent (the former referee) dies (and leaves the ring). When money is involved, it's every man (or woman) for himself.

40 Leave specific bequests greater than your residuary estate.

A specific bequest is a sum of money or a particular item of property (real or personal) to be distributed to a specific person or persons. For example, "I leave the sum of $100,000 to each of my four (4) grandchildren." Great idea, in theory, provided you actually have at least $400,000 as part of your probate or trust estate that can be left to your grandchildren.

Suppose you have added a second owner to all your assets or have a designated beneficiary for your assets. As a result, there are no or limited assets actually governed by your written estate plan. In that case, there will be nothing to distribute to your grandchildren. Zip, zero, zilch. Nothing. Think this doesn't happen; think again. It happens every day.

And, if you do leave sufficient assets for the specific bequests but with the idea that the beneficiaries of your "residuary estate" - everything that's left over after all debts and specific bequests have been satisfied - will receive the balance of your estate, your residuary beneficiaries may be in for a big surprise! Sometimes, the residuary beneficiaries who were intended to receive most of the estate end up with the smallest portion or nothing at all in the worst case. Here's an example. The decedent has an estate worth $300,000. The Last Will makes specific gifts to four grandchildren of $100,000 each. First, there isn't even enough to make the gifts to the grandkids because legal fees and creditor claims get paid first. Second, the gifts to the grandkids will be reduced on a pro-rata basis. The children who were named to get the balance (residuary) of the estate actually end up with zero. Tough day for them.

41 Fail to specifically disinherit people you don't like.

If you specifically intend to disinherit someone, it's better to say so than to say nothing. Saying nothing opens the door for a straight-faced argument that you may have inadvertently left them out. A very specific, "I have intentionally not provided for Greedy Gary and his descendants" leaves no room for interpretation. You don't have to say why. Just be blunt and say they get nothing.

This is also true for identifying who your "final beneficiaries" are. If you don't name specific beneficiaries that "take" in the event all of your primary beneficiaries are deceased, the law of the state where you live will leave it to your "heirs at law." These are the people that are most closely related to you.

If you don't want your brother, sister, niece, nephew, father, mother, etc., to become an accidental beneficiary, best to include that information in your Last Will or Living Trust. Better yet, name a charity as your final beneficiary. The probability of this final beneficiary actually receiving something is small but better safe than sorry.

42 Leave a person $1 instead of disinheriting them.

People think leaving a person a dollar ($1), similar to leaving a penny to a poor waitress or waiter, to prove a point is recommended. It is not. There may be some attorneys that disagree with me, but I'm willing to take that risk.

Sometimes professionals disagree.

If you leave someone a dollar (or a de minimis amount like $10 or $100), that person is a rightful beneficiary, and you have likely invited them to the party that will become a lawsuit. (Remember what happens when families fight? Lawyers win.). As a named beneficiary, they are now entitled to notice of all estate proceedings, including a copy of the Last Will, an inventory of all estate assets, and a periodic accounting. The person you intended to disinherit can now make the lives of all your other beneficiaries miserable and cost your estate thousands in unexpected attorneys fees. The "disinherited" person will likely stir the pot continuously, an outcome you did not intend.

43 Count on joint tenancy to avoid probate.

Joint tenancy is a form of ownership where two or more people own an asset together. There are different types of joint tenancy.

There are tenants in common (TIC) where each owner has a specific percentage ownership interest in the property. This type of joint tenancy actually guarantees probate. You own your percentage individually, and it is governed by your Last Will (or lack thereof). Sometimes people get confused and think that TIC is the same as joint tenants with rights of survivorship. Unfortunately, they usually learn this lesson the hard way.

Then there are joint tenants with rights of survivorship (sometimes referred to as JTWROS) where when the first owner dies, the survivor owns that person's interest. The interest passes by operation of law without probate. So, this is one way to avoid probate, but only temporarily. A probate will still be required at the death of the second owner.

The last type of joint ownership is tenants by the entirety (TBE). This form of ownership is only available to married couples. State law requires that certain "unities" be present when this type of ownership is created for it to be valid. When the first spouse dies, the survivor owns the entire property by operation of law. In addition to avoiding probate at the death of the first to die, TBE can also provide creditor protection as it requires both owners to be sued for the property to be attached as part of the lawsuit.

The fallacy in joint tenancy where there is a survivorship feature is the idea that you can avoid probate. Well, you can, but only temporarily until the second owner dies. Probate applies to assets owned individually, without a named beneficiary. After the death of the first joint owner, the asset is individually owned unless you go to great lengths to add new joint owners continuously. In the event of simultaneous death, most state laws will treat the property as being owned 50% by each owner, and the asset will be subject to probate in both estates.

Avoiding probate should never be your only estate planning goal. Your trusted legal advisor can provide you with the pros and cons of each form of ownership as it relates to your particular situation.

44 Rely on ownership or beneficiary designations without a backup plan.

This mistake is similar to the fallacy of joint ownership with rights of survivorship but with the added component of beneficiary designations. Naming a beneficiary on an asset governed by contract (life insurance, a bank account, an annuity, a retirement plan, etc.) may meet your goal of avoiding probate. That is if your intended beneficiary doesn't die before you do, and then you fail to update your designation.

It is recommended to name primary, secondary, and in some cases, tertiary (3 sets) of beneficiaries. That way, if the first-named beneficiary is not living or should disclaim (a legal no thank you) their interest, there are alternate takers for the asset.

If you fail to name a beneficiary or your beneficiary designation is rejected for any reason, then the terms of the contract that govern that asset will likely have a scheme of distribution built in. The contract beneficiaries may be your heirs - your spouse, then your kids, etc., or it could be your estate.

If your estate becomes your beneficiary, probate is guaranteed, and your goal of avoiding probate was not accomplished. If your spouse, kids, or others become your beneficiaries, you may have avoided probate. But, depending on your goals for those beneficiaries, there may be a complete failure of your estate plan. And if one or more of these family members are people you didn't want to receive a benefit from your estate, then the joke's on you. They win.

Remember, a named beneficiary receives the asset outright, free from all of the planning you may have done to protect the beneficiary (minority, special needs, divorce, creditors, drug/alcohol/gambling addictions, just to name a few). If you did planning and created trusts to benefit those you love, then the trust needs to be the beneficiary of your asset, not the people.

45 Not include or improperly use a no-contest clause.

A "no-contest" clause, also referred to as an *in terrorem* clause provides that if a beneficiary or other person should contest the provisions of your Last Will or Living Trust, they run the risk of being disinherited. However, If they weren't a beneficiary anyway because they were explicitly disinherited, they may have nothing to lose.

Sometimes a no-contest clause is referred to as "paper tiger." It may discourage litigation based on the potential of harsh results. No-contest clauses are not valid in all jurisdictions yet may still be included for their ability to scare off litigation.

Here are some possible outcomes when using a no-contest clause. The first is if you leave a beneficiary nothing and they challenge, they have nothing to lose because they weren't going to receive anything anyway. This really doesn't compute for me because if you leave them nothing and they challenge, they still end up with nothing. Or, perhaps they will challenge the planning on the theory that they might get something and something is better than nothing. Or, they may hope to invalidate the existing planning in favor of a prior plan or even intestacy.

Perhaps the better suggestion is to say if they challenge the planning, they will only get a $1? Isn't litigation fun?

You will want to check your state's rules to see if a no-contest clause is valid and consult with a professional to see if it makes sense for your estate plan.

46 Leave exempt assets to the wrong beneficiaries.

State probate statutes generally identify specific assets that are exempt from the claims of creditors. In some cases, these assets are exempt only if left to certain people, typically family members who are blood relatives. As a result, if you leave an exempt asset to a non-family member, that asset may no longer be exempt. If the asset is not exempt, it will be subject to the claims of estate creditors, and the asset's value to the beneficiary will be diminished.

Florida homestead is a specific creditor exempt asset. When a Florida homestead is left to a spouse or heir, the proceeds from the sale of that asset are exempt from the claims of the deceased's creditors. However, if the property is left to a friend or non-relative (like a charity), it doesn't enjoy the same creditor protection.

This can be particularly problematic if you leave a portion to an "exempt person" and a portion to a "non-exempt" person. The non-exempt person ends up having their portion subject to the creditor claim, reducing the amount they receive.

In some states, there are restrictions on the persons to whom you can leave specific property. Florida has a constitutional restriction on the devise and descent of homestead property. If the deceased is survived by a spouse or a minor child, the law determines how that property will descend. The result is often at odds with what the deceased would have wanted if they were aware of the complication they just created.

Here's an example. The deceased owns his homestead property in his individual name. He dies without a Last Will. He is survived by a spouse and adult children from a previous marriage, but no minor children. The law provides that his spouse has a choice - 1. She can receive the property as the life tenant (with full rights to reside on the property or rent it) with the remainder interest to the lineal heirs of the deceased; or 2. She can elect a fifty percent (50%) ownership interest as tenants in common with the lineal heirs owning the other fifty percent (50%). Which to choose? It's usually a math problem. Sometimes, the decision can turn on whether the surviving spouse intends to reside on the property or intends to sell it.

In our case at hand, the lineal heirs of the deceased have been difficult to identify. Initially, we believed there were four (4) surviving daughters. Then, a man claiming to be the adopted son of the deceased emerged. Now there are five (5) potential beneficiaries. The appearance of the adopted son caused one of the children to question whether the fact that two of her sisters had been adopted by another man would affect the outcome? Absolutely. In most cases, the adoption of a child by another person terminates their inheritance rights from the biological parent. So, it appears that we now have only three (3) lineal heirs. Ain't life fun?

47 Trigger estate taxes with life insurance.

The number one thing life insurance salespersons are taught about life insurance and its proceeds are they are free from income tax. What they sometimes fail to realize is they are not free from estate tax. The death benefit of a life insurance policy is included in the deceased's estate if he owned that policy at the time of his death. Remember, your taxable estate includes everything you own, everything you control, and everything your name is on. In the case of a life insurance policy, if you own it or control it, the death benefit is included in your taxable estate. If you own a life insurance policy on another person with accumulated cash value, the cash value is included in your taxable estate for estate tax purposes.

There are strategies for owning life insurance, so the death benefit proceeds are not included in the insured's taxable estate. Be sure to work with your trusted legal and financial advisors to learn how the proceeds can be excluded from your taxable estate.

48 **Not understand how retirement plan beneficiaries get maximum stretch out or take advantage of trust provisions.**

A commonly misunderstood area of the law is how retirement plan beneficiaries interact with estate planning. Financial advisors are taught to never name a trust as a beneficiary of a retirement plan. What!? Some individuals are not appropriate for outright beneficiary designations.

These are the people you've likely done trust planning for so you can provide them with ongoing supervision, guidance, or protection. If you name these same individuals as the outright beneficiary of a retirement plan, then you've wasted your time and your money creating a trust for their benefit.

Trusts can be legal beneficiaries of a retirement plan. There are specific rules that have to be followed, but seasoned estate planning professionals should be aware of these rules and ensure they are included in your trust plan.

Naming an outright beneficiary on any asset is a complete loss of control when you die. That individual can do anything they want with that asset and are not bound by any terms and conditions (such as those that may be in a trust.) They can spend the money any way they want and can leave the asset to anyone they want. If they are receiving government benefits, they may lose their eligibility. If they are irresponsible with money, kiss that money goodbye. If they are your second spouse and leave the asset to their children instead of yours, well, that's on you. You chose the wrong beneficiary.

The "stretch out" provisions of the law regarding retirement plan beneficiaries allow for the continued tax deferral of that asset. For example, a surviving spouse can "stretch out" the retirement plan distributions over their life expectancy. The same may be true for certain other classes of beneficiaries, including special needs persons. The stretch out rules are subject to change, and they recently did change, reducing the number of years a retirement plan can be deferred for particular beneficiaries.

The stretch out concept is admirable - it allows a beneficiary to continue the tax deferral of that retirement plan. Realistically, your desire that your beneficiary defers the income tax on that asset may not be achieved. If the beneficiary has the right to claim the full distribution of that asset on request, they might be willing to pay the tax just to get to the bigger lump sum benefit now.

In some states, the beneficiaries of a retirement plan may enjoy creditor protection. However, if your beneficiaries don't live in the same state as you do, that protection may be forfeited. Always meet with your tax, financial and legal professionals to explore all of your retirement plan options.

49 Plan your estate around specific assets - bank accounts, financial assets, or properties that don't exist or may result in unequal or unintended distributions.
Families love to fight. They especially love to fight over stuff. They love to fight over unequal distributions. When you leave specific financial assets, collectibles, or other one-of-a-kind items that you've either sold during your lifetime or given to someone else, that's a good reason for a fight, a lawsuit or a very long grudge.

If you've given away an item of sentimental or actual value to the person who thought they were supposed to receive it or who was intended to receive it in a written instrument, the recipient may not take this oversight lightly.

It's not a good idea to identify specific accounts or a specific number of shares of an investment to individually named beneficiaries. This can be very dangerous. If the account is no longer in existence, then the beneficiary will not receive their intended inheritance. If the value of the specific assets vary and your goal is to treat beneficiaries equally, that may not work either.

I once had a mom who meticulously kept records of all her investments. She had each of her children named as a beneficiary on each asset. She kept them lined up in columns measuring the monthly changes in their values so that each child would get an equal distribution. She wanted to avoid probate - a goal, but not the end game.

There are at least 101 ways this type of planning can go wrong. What happens if mom ends up in the hospital, rehab, or nursing home and needs to spend her money at a time when she is unable to keep up with her complex system of keeping the pile of money for each child equal? Someone gets the short end of the stick. Far better to make a Last Will and own everything in her individual name, or create a Living Trust and title assets in the name of the trust, and then leave all of her assets to her children equally. Or, at the very least, put all the children as a beneficiary on every asset.

50 Fail to consider who pays the estate taxes that will be due.

If you have a taxable estate, one that will be subject to a hefty estate tax, not only do you have to consider the liquidity of the funds required to pay the tax, you have to make sure you haven't accidentally placed the burden of paying the tax on unsuspecting beneficiaries.

Assets left to a U.S. citizen spouse utilize the unlimited marital deduction and are not subject to estate tax at the first spouse's death. If you leave assets to a non-spouse that are subject to tax, you also have to consider who will be responsible for the tax payment and from what source those funds will be found.

A client owns several business interests and lots of real property. His estate will be taxable regardless of how high the estate tax exemption gets (unless it is unlimited). He wants to leave 60% of his estate to his spouse (his 4th wife) and the remaining 40% to his children. They will bear the burden of the estate tax on these assets. The assets are not liquid - they are ongoing business interests and real property. Where will the funds come from to pay the tax? The children do not have the personal means to pay the tax. The only source for the tax payment is from the assets themselves, which will have to be sold at fire-sale prices so that the tax can be paid nine (9) months after the date of death.

What are some possible solutions? He could buy a life insurance policy to create liquidity. If he buys it in his individual name, it will also be subject to estate tax. He could buy it in an irrevocable life insurance trust (ILIT) to remove it from his estate for estate tax purposes. Ultimately, he needs to be insurable - he's over 70, and he has to be willing to pay the premium (not an insignificant amount) for the remainder of his life to ensure the policy will be in force at the relevant time.

He could sell all of his illiquid investments during his lifetime. This is actually his goal, but even the best-laid plans go awry. He's not in any hurry to sell because the assets are performing well. He believes he will have "enough time" before he dies to make the sale. This plan works if you know when you are going to die and can plan ahead.

He could engage in some other advanced planning strategies, but I already know from meeting with him and his CPA he is not open to these suggestions. As a result, he will likely take no action and his heirs will be left to figure it out when he dies.

51 Fail to consider the income tax consequences of your planning.

Not all assets are treated equally. Any time you leave someone an asset you have not paid income tax on, such as a retirement plan or tax-deferred annuity, the person you are leaving it to gets the privilege of paying the income tax.

As a result, leaving your daughter a $100,000 investment account with stocks and bonds and leaving your son a $100,000 Individual Retirement Account (IRA) is not the same. Your daughter gets the $100,000 free from income tax (she got a step up in basis on the date of your death, so there are no capital gains taxes), but your son receives the IRA as personal income on which he will have to pay taxes. Depending on his tax bracket, that could result in a hefty decrease in his inherited gift.

52 Use the wrong assets to fund a gift to charity.

This is similar to not considering the income tax consequences of a gift. The best assets to leave to charity are assets on which you have not paid income tax.

Charitable organizations are exempt from income tax. If you leave your $100,000 Individual Retirement Account (IRA) to a charity, the charity will receive the entire benefit of that gift. At death, always choose tax-deferred assets as the best gifts for charitable organizations. For lifetime gifts, choose assets with built-in capital gains like low basis stock or real property investments.

The charity will not be subject to the capital gains tax or the income tax.

If you plan to create and fund a Charitable Remainder Trust (CRT) during your lifetime, these same rules apply. Choose assets that have built-in gains.

53 Fail to use charitable planning as a way to avoid estate taxes.

No one has to pay estate tax. If you are charitably minded, you can always leave assets to charity as a way to avoid the estate tax entirely or take some of the bite out of the estate tax.

You can make direct gifts to charity at your death for all assets that would be subject to estate tax. You can create a Testamentary Charitable Lead Trust (TCLAT) designed to zero out the estate tax after paying a stream of income to a charity for a sufficiently long time to avoid estate tax. You can leave assets subject to tax to a Family Foundation to create a family legacy and promote family philanthropy.

There are many ways to use charitable gifts and charitable planning to avoid the payment of estate tax. You simply have to choose your charity - do you want to leave assets to the United States government to be spent at its discretion, or do you want to choose your philanthropic endeavors? Ultimately, the choice is yours.

54 Miss the disclaimer deadline for a tax-qualified disclaimer.

A disclaimer is a form of "legal no thank you." The intended recipient of a gift can "refuse" the gift so that it passes to the next beneficiary in line. A properly executed disclaimer is not a gift from the person disclaiming the gift (the disclaimant) for gift tax purposes (but beware, this may not be true for Medicaid planning purposes.). This type of disclaimer is referred to as a tax-qualified disclaimer, and it must be executed within nine months of the date of the death of the decedent in order to be effective.

It is important to note that if you are the intended recipient of a gift and execute a valid disclaimer, you DO NOT get to choose where the gift or bequest goes next. The gift would descend to the person who would have received the gift if you had been deceased. As a result, it is important to consult with a legal and tax professional before executing any disclaimer.

55 Have a Trust without a Last Will.
When you have a Trust, you still need a Last Will. "Why?" you say. Because it is almost 100% guaranteed that not all of your assets will be titled in the name of your Trust by the time you die. There will be some asset that ends up unexpectedly in your probate estate.

Probate assets are governed either by state law or by your Last Will. Most Last Wills that work in connection with a Trust are referred to as "Pour Over Wills." This is because their job is to pour assets from the probate estate to the trust estate. The Trust is where your primary set of instructions are and where your beneficiaries are named.

The Pour Over Will has a couple of possible functions. One is to name your Trust as the beneficiary of your probate estate. Another is to nominate your Personal Representative/Executor. Another is to appoint guardians for minor children.

If you've neglected to execute a Pour Over Will and there are assets in your probate estate, they will be distributed to your statutory heirs at law. Of all the reasons you need to have a Last Will to avoid unintended consequences and unexpected beneficiaries, this is another one. Imagine if you should happen to die under circumstances where your estate becomes the recipient of a significant sum of money from a wrongful death suit. Now, instead of those assets being distributed according to the terms of your Trust, your intestate heirs will be your unintended beneficiaries.

56 Be a cheapskate.
An estate plan prepared by a professional is not going to be free. There are costs associated with any kind of professional advice. You've heard the saying, "You get what you pay for." Nothing could be more true when it comes to estate planning. Don't do your own estate planning. Don't have a friend of a friend who is a criminal attorney do your estate planning. Don't choose the cheapest provider of estate plans you can find. This is not the time to be "penny-wise and pound-foolish." There's too much riding on the results.

I love the saying, "If you think a professional is expensive, try an amateur." There are lots of well-meaning (and some not so well-meaning) individuals out there "selling" estate plans. Find a reputable professional you feel comfortable with that teaches you the questions you didn't know to ask and makes the process enjoyable and understandable.

57 Think your state plan is "simple."
There's no such thing as a "simple" estate plan. In fact, when potential clients tell me their plan is simple, I reply, "My fee has just doubled." I know from experience there is no such thing as a simple estate plan. There are likely complexities you haven't even considered that will be discovered as you go through the planning process.

The law is complex. There is no way your plan is simple. You will have family dynamic concerns, relationship concerns, asset concerns, tax concerns, etc., that will impact how your plan will be created and implemented.

58 Don't care what happens when you die.

You don't have to care; I can't make you. However, if you don't care what happens when you die, there will undoubtedly be unexpected results and consequences. You may actually enjoy sitting on your cloud watching the chaos unfold around your family, loved ones, friends, and pets.

You might not care, but those that care about you will.

59 Fail to include an "atomic bomb" plan.

An atomic bomb plan, or in Florida, a "salmonella family picnic" provision is the final, final beneficiary of your estate plan, also called a remote contingent beneficiary. This means that if all of your named beneficiaries and their descendants are no longer living, who will be the recipient of your estate? In most estate plans, the likelihood of this occurrence is pretty small, but we all learned from the events of September 11, 2001, those small probability events can and do happen.

As a result, don't spend too much time thinking about this portion of your estate plan, but do think about where you would want your assets to go if your intended beneficiaries are unavailable. This is a good place to think about naming a charitable beneficiary. If you fail to name a remote contingent beneficiary, your state of residence will "fill in the blank" for you, and your "heirs at law" will become your final beneficiary.

CHAPTER TWO

Tips for Individuals/ Single People

This section is specific to those individuals who are single and not in a committed relationship with a married or unmarried partner. There are subsequent sections to address the estate planning issues that arise when in a relationship. This section may apply to the young or old but will specifically address the concerns of the single person.

1 **Think you are too young to have an estate plan.**
If you have attained the age of majority (generally 18), then you are old enough to have an estate plan. This is true even if you think you don't have an estate, which you might not, yet. However, you cannot predict what will happen in your life. You may be in an accident that results in your inability to make your own financial or healthcare-related decisions. Without a plan, your parents will

not have the legal authority to make those decisions for you, and you might find yourself in a guardianship.

As an adult, the world assumes you are capable of making all of your own decisions, good or bad. If you are involved in an accident whereby you lose your ability to make decisions, there is no automatic right for your parents to make decisions for you. Without a written estate plan delegating decision-making authority, your parents will be forced to pursue a guardianship and petition a court for two things; 1. A determination of incapacity, and 2. An appointment of a legal guardian for financial decision-making and a legal guardian for health care decision-making.

2 Think only married people need an estate plan.

Estate planning isn't only for married people, people with kids, or older people. Estate planning is for everyone. Everyone has an estate plan, like it or not. If you are a single person and you die without an estate plan, the state where you live will determine who gets your assets. This could be your parents, your siblings, your nieces/nephews, or more distant relatives. It will certainly not include your life partner, beloved friends, a pet, or favorite charity. When the state determines your beneficiaries, you have lost complete control over the disposition of your estate. If your attitude is, "Heck, I don't care, I'm dead," then no worries. If you do care, get a plan.

3 Name friends as beneficiaries.

This can be an estate planning mistake if the person or persons you've named are no longer your friends. Friends come in three varieties - those in your life for a season, a reason, or a lifetime. Lifetime friends are few and far between. Those that are in our life for a short time are more common. Leaving them your estate without constantly reviewing and updating your legal documents, asset ownership, and beneficiary designations can result in some really unexpected results.

I remember a client who named a now-former girlfriend as the beneficiary of his trust. Their relationship ended in a bad way, even including a temporary restraining order. However, he failed to update his estate planning, and when he died, his Successor Trustee was required to give her the assets he left her.

4 Rely on state law to distribute assets to your parents.

Without a written, legal estate plan, your parents are likely your default beneficiaries if you are a single person. This may be fine, but it could be a disaster depending on the quality of your relationship with your parents and your desire to have them inherit your estate.

If your parents are divorced, and your relationship with one of your parents has deteriorated, this fact is irrelevant if you die without a Last Will. If your parent has remarried and becomes your beneficiary, their new spouse could also end up as your beneficiary.

Unintended beneficiaries happen all the time. Sometimes, even when you do have a plan. One client who died left everything to her son in her Last Will. Unfortunately, her son died 32 days after she died. Under the terms of her Last Will, he only had to survive her for 30 days to be her beneficiary. He lived long enough to be her beneficiary. However, he did not have an estate plan, so his estate (and the estate he just inherited from his mother) went one-half to his estranged spouse (a second wife) and one-half to his three children (one from the first marriage and two from the second). That is a result I'm sure his mother never expected or intended!

CHAPTER THREE

Tips for Parents

This section applies to persons who have children. These can be young children or adult children. You can be a married person or a single person - the common denominator is that you have a child that you may (or may not) want to plan for. Some jurisdictions will protect your children, even if you don't. Others will create legal outcomes that may be inconsistent with your long-term goals for your children.

1 Not having life insurance to protect your children if you die prematurely.

No one expects to die. In fact, we all seem to expect that instead, we will win the lottery. News flash, you will die, and you are not likely to win the lottery. If you have children that rely on you for support, then life insurance is the most cost-effective way to ensure they will continue to have that support when you die.

The saddest stories are those where the primary wage earner parent died and left the family without a means of support. Or where the caregiver parent died, and now the wage earner parent has sole responsibility for providing the care and support of the children. A life insurance policy can provide the resources necessary to allow the wage earner parent the luxury of continuing to provide excellent care for their children. The life insurance proceeds can be used to engage a caregiver for the kids, provide for home care, shopping, meal preparation, essentially all of the services the caregiver parent provides.

I frequently see couples where the primary wage earner is insured because they have life insurance through their employer. They never considered getting a life insurance policy on the caregiver spouse because they never thought about what life would look like if that person were unable to provide the caregiving.

When both parents work, it isn't unusual for one of them to comment, "I could use a wife." We all need the assistance of an extra set of hands, an extra brain, more time in our day, etc.

2 Name your minor children as beneficiaries of your retirement plan or life insurance.

Just as a Last Will guarantees probate, naming your minor children as beneficiaries of your retirement plan or life insurance guarantees guardianship. Minors under the age of majority (younger than 18) generally cannot own and likely, shouldn't be managing assets they inherit. The state default when a child inherits assets is a guardianship of the property. This is a court-administered process for overseeing the management of the child's assets until they reach the age of majority.

The primary candidate as guardian of the property for a minor is the surviving biological parent. This may not be your intended outcome if that person is your former spouse or the last person on the planet you would want managing assets for the benefit of your kids.

One of the saddest and most disturbing cases I was involved in was a young mother who had spent years fighting with her former spouse over custody of her son. It was a bitter, angry, expensive, and emotionally devastating battle. In a moment of despair, the young mother took her life by suicide. She did not have a Last Will.

In the middle of the night, with cops in tow, the biological father showed up on the grandparents' doorstep and demanded his right as the father to custody of his child. This was terrifying and emotionally destructive for the child (not to minimize the devastation to the grandparents). In addition, the child was the sole heir of his mother's estate. However, as a child, he could not legally own and control these assets. His father had the legal right to become the guardian of the child's property. The final result was the complete opposite of everything the mother had spent so many years trying to avoid.

When a minor attains the age of majority, the assets held in a guardianship of the property for their benefit are released to the now young adult person. This person may not have the aptitude, maturity, life experience, etc., to manage these assets without supervision. They may have a troubled life affected by drugs, alcohol, or other concerns. These issues are likely irrelevant as the court must distribute the assets to the young adult based solely on attaining the age of majority.

Small amounts of money in the hands of a young, inexperienced person can have disastrous results. If you want to control the distribution of assets for your children, you need to have a plan that contemplates a trust for their benefit that will distribute assets at a time when they are more financially mature or in a way that will allow them to benefit from the assets without ruining their life.

3 **Think you can decide that someone other than your former spouse will be the legal guardian of your child(ren).**
The biological parent of a child has legal rights regarding custody of the child. This is true unless parental rights have been terminated (voluntarily or involuntarily). The fact that you think your parents, your new spouse, your family or your friends would be a better choice doesn't matter. You can express an opinion as to who should be the proper guardian of the person and have custody of your child, but ultimately, the court and the law will prevail.

You CAN control who manages the assets (guardian of the property or Trustee) for the benefit of your children. And, this is an excellent reason to do your planning as a parent so that you remain in control of who will be responsible for the assets left for the benefit of your child.

4 **Put your child's name on your assets.**
There are many reasons why this may not be a good idea, regardless of your child's age. Naming a minor as a joint owner is never a good idea. The same is true with naming a minor as a beneficiary. Naming an adult child as a joint owner has a lot of possible negative side effects; a complete loss of control of that asset in the event of your death, exposure to the claims of your child's creditors, misuse of the assets by your child, loss of step-up in basis, gift tax, just to name a few.

You will likely be better served by having an estate plan or long-term care asset protection plan that considers all of the possible negative side effects of naming others as joint owners of your assets.

5 Become estranged from your biological and/or adopted children.

When you are estranged from your children, they are still your legal heirs. This is true even if you have not spoken to them since they were young children, and now they are grown-up adults.

Biological and adopted children generally have the same inheritance rights. For all intents and purposes, they are your children with all of the attendant rights associated with that family relationship. The best way to successfully disinherit your legal heirs is to create an estate plan and specifically disinherit those persons you do not want to inherit your estate.

6 Fail to recognize that your stepchildren are not your legal heirs.

If you love your stepchildren, you need to intentionally provide for them as part of your estate plan. They are not automatically your legal heirs just because you are married to their biological parent.

Here's an example. A man has three children from a first marriage. He and his first wife divorced. He marries wife number two, who has three children of her own. These children are very young at the time of the marriage, and the man raises them with love and affection. In fact, with more love and affection than he gave to his biological children from the first marriage, who he was estranged from.

His second wife predeceased him. When he died unexpectedly without a Last Will, all six children had expectations about how they would share his estate. The stepchildren assumed the biological children would want nothing to do with his estate because they had wanted nothing to do with their father. Remember what happens when you "assume" anything. The biological children were VERY interested in his estate and were his only legal heirs. The stepchildren ended up with no legal rights and no entitlement to any portion of his estate. The result is a lot of hurt feelings and unintended consequences.

7 Assume your kids will get along after you die.

I hope you have a family where everyone loves everyone all the time. However, if your family is like most, the kids don't always get along. And, when the parent (also known as "the referee") leaves the ring, you can count on some unexpected battles.

As you know, money always brings out the best in people - LOL! Kids will fight over anything, including the dumbest things you can think of. Splitting up a parent's estate can be similar to a divorce. There are a lot of turf wars. There are lots of unresolved feelings that have developed over a long time.

Sibling rivalry is not uncommon, even in the best of families. Expect that your children will not get along; plan for the worst and hope for the best. Don't create situations where you open the door for conflict between or among your children.

Consider engaging the services of a professional fiduciary so that one of your children is not nominated as the sole individual responsible for the administration of your estate. Sometimes parents want to name all of their kids to act together to administer an estate. This sounds fair but can create all kinds of conflict and often ends in all sides "lawyering up."

Some kids do not have the organizational skills, the acumen, the stick-to-it-tiveness that estate administration requires. Forcing them into this role is not going to miraculously give them these skills. Forcing children to work together after your death when they couldn't get along during your lifetime is a recipe for disaster.

8 Treat unequals as equals.

Children are not created equally. Yet, what all typical kids really want is to be treated equally. In a typical family, this would be my recommendation. In a family with a child who has special needs, the solution may require a different answer. An individual with special needs may require special planning that contemplates that this person's needs may be greater than the needs of the other, more capable, neuro-typical children.

Suppose your family resources are limited, and you have a child with special needs. In that case, your circumstances may dictate that you leave a greater percentage of your assets in a special needs trust for the benefit of your special person. This may be especially true if the nature of the disability affects the individual's ability to earn a living and they have a normal life expectancy.

Sometimes parents feel that one or more of their children should receive a greater percentage of the assets because they are more successful than the others. Before making that decision to treat the more successful child unequally, raise the proposed distribution scheme in a family conversation and see what kind of response you get.

I represented a family where there were four children. The parents were doctors. Three of the four kids were doctors, and the fourth child was married to a doctor. They were all doing pretty well.

Except, one of the kids became a single mother and was diagnosed with cancer. Her ability to provide for her family was no longer on the same level as her siblings. The parents determined they would leave her a greater percentage of their assets since she had more life challenges than the others. When the parents brought up this solution at a holiday gathering, they got an unexpected response. All of the children wanted to be treated equally, despite their different life circumstances.

In my experience, this is a very common and typical response. The more successful siblings were unwilling to be generous to their "struggling" sister; the parents were stunned. To level the playing field, based on the kids' response, the parents devised a distribution plan that would require each of the kids to submit their annual tax returns reflecting their earnings. Then there would be an estate distribution to "equalize" the respective incomes of each of the children. Creative and genius, but likely this plan will not get the warm reception the parents expect.

Parents always want to help those that need their help the most. Kids don't always appreciate this sentiment as sometimes the kids who need the most help have received that "help" on an ongoing basis throughout their lifetime. This form of lifetime favoritism can create resentment among the kids that feel they didn't receive the same consideration, regardless of their capabilities. You know your family best.

9 Leave children unequal distributions.

Sometimes parents attempt to "punish" their children by disinheriting a child or leaving unequal distributions. There may be very good reasons to do this but do this only with the expectation it may create future problems.

Conflict will be inevitable if there is a perception that an estate plan was changed

or modified because the child receiving the larger share was exerting "undue influence" over the parent. In this instance, there will be several factors that will be considered in a legal battle. Some of these factors will include whether the child receiving the larger share was responsible for taking the parent to the lawyer; whether the child was present during the consultation with the lawyer; whether the child maintains custody of the estate planning documents, to name a few.

It is not unusual for a lawyer who suspects undue influence or is being cautious to request that children not be present during the consultation, so there is no appearance of impropriety or undue influence. This is not an insult to the child; it is to ensure that the decision being made by the parent is made of their own volition without any input from the present child.

10 Leave your assets to your "descendants."

The definition of the term descendants can be confusing. Is it just your children, or does it also include your grandchildren, great-grandchildren, and so on? Does the use of the term descendants create ambiguity in your estate plan that will require a Petition to Determine Beneficiaries to ensure that all persons entitled to inherit have the opportunity to be represented and to have "their day in court?"

Lawyers love definitions. Make sure if you use a defined term that it means what you think it means. Otherwise, your estate could end up in litigation.

11 Choose the wrong guardian for your child.

I was having lunch with a friend who had done her planning where she named a guardian for her minor child. She commented she may have chosen the wrong guardian because her son would be better served, in his life and as a person, being raised by another family who has a child his age and share similar family values, rather than go to her sister.

Selecting a guardian for minor children can be one of the biggest disagreements among parents. Who is the best choice? Sometimes my answer is, "You don't have to agree; you just have to live longer." Ultimately, the choice of guardian in your estate plan is only relevant if: 1. Both parents die at the same time or 2. Before the child turns 18. Essentially, you are planning for a low probability event, which likely won't happen, but there has to be a plan.

Failure to choose a guardian is worse than not choosing one at all. If you don't make your preference known for the guardian for your minor child, then the court will make that decision for you based on statutory preferences. You will make the better choice.

Choose a guardian that will teach your child the same values you would teach them. You don't have to choose family members just because they are family. Sometimes close friends are a better choice.

CHAPTER FOUR

Tips for Unmarried Couples

This section is specifically directed to those persons who are in a committed but unmarried relationship. Technically you are two single people that may have estate planning goals that resemble married persons. Yet, the law in most jurisdictions does not recognize the legal status of an unmarried couple and will treat most unmarried persons as legal strangers. Unmarried couples have to create legal structures that provide them with the legal protections they desire.

1 **Fail to have a written plan regarding a division of assets in the event the relationship ends - Life Alliance Agreement™.**

Lots of people live in unmarried relationships. Marriage may be on the horizon - someday, it may seem too restrictive or may not be "your cup of tea." However, both short and long-term committed relationships can and do end, just like marital relationships.

Unfortunately, there is no set of "divorce" laws to protect the splitting up of unmarried couples. Legally, unmarried couples are strangers to one another. You have no more rights than an unknown person you meet on the street.

Relationships can end for a variety of reasons that may include irreconcilable differences or death. I particularly hate the call that asks, "My partner just died without a Last Will; what are my rights?" Short answer - none.

The same is true if the relationship ends and there is no contemplation for how the assets acquired by the two of you will be divided. The biggest fights I've seen have been over real property and pets. It is not unusual for an unmarried couple to invest jointly in a piece of property that may be owned by only one of the partners. Without an agreement, at the termination of the relationship, the one who owns the property may end up with all of the benefits. There may be an argument for "unjust enrichment," but that requires a lawsuit, the resources to mount and defend the lawsuit, and a judge that agrees with that outcome.

The same is true for pets. If you jointly acquire a pet, it is well-advised to create a written agreement that determines who will be the pet's legal owner, how custody of the pet may be shared, and how the ongoing expenses of the pet will be determined. Courts and state laws are not well-equipped to handle disputes related to pets and their custody, despite the fact we consider them to be our "children who wear fur coats."

Unmarried couples have to create their own protections. This includes entering into a written agreement - I call them Life Alliance Agreements™ - where you outline how the relationship and the division of assets will be handled if the relationship ends. Both parties must obtain separate legal representation and completely disclose all financial assets. This will avoid possible claims of one partner taking advantage of another in the future.

See my book, "Loving Without a License" and "Whether To Wed" by Scott Squillace for more information. Both are available on Amazon.

2 Own assets jointly with your partner.

Sometimes couples think it is a good idea to acquire and own assets jointly either as tenants in common or as joint tenants with rights of survivorship. This might include real property, bank accounts, vehicles, etc. Whether this is a good idea or not depends. This is a typical lawyer answer, but it's true. It depends on the relationship. And, it depends on the contribution of the individual partners.

In some instances, one partner contributes the lion's share of the resources to the acquisition and/or maintenance of an asset. In the event of a dissolution of the relationship, jointly held assets will generally be divided equally. This will be true regardless of the individual contribution of each partner.

If assets are owned jointly, they may also be subject to the claims of one of the owner's creditors. There is no marital protection of assets owned jointly by unmarried partners.

Joint ownership can be a way to avoid probate, but it can create problems when it comes to the dissolution of the relationship for a reason other than death. If you acquire assets jointly with another person, be sure you understand all of the possible ramifications.

3 Fail to give your partner legal rights with regard to healthcare decisions or visitation in the event you become ill.

A life partner is a relative stranger to you from a legal standpoint. They don't have any statutory rights to make healthcare-related decisions for you. This can have devastating results if the unexpected happens.

A close friend was in an unmarried relationship. They hoped to be married, but that day had not arrived. They had not contemplated doing comprehensive estate planning to provide legal authority for the other to make important life decisions. When the male partner unexpectedly suffered a severe and ultimately fatal health event, my friend found herself in a position where she could not make any healthcare-related decisions for him. In fact, his family eventually barred her from even visiting him or expressing an opinion regarding his care and the provision of life-prolonging procedures. When he died, she was devastated. The experience was beyond anything she could have comprehended.

If you want your partner to be able to make healthcare decisions for you, along with having access to you for visitation purposes, you MUST create these protections for yourself. The law will not do it for you.

4 Assume it is better to be single than married.

I made this assumption for a long time. My husband, Joe, and I were in an unmarried but committed relationship for fourteen (14) years before we got married. In fact, it took my writing the book "Loving Without a License" to convince me that we would be better off legally as a married couple.

There are approximately 1,100 benefits - both state and federal - that are acquired when you get married. I call this the "unexpected wedding gift." I couldn't even come close to telling you what all of these benefits are, but many of them revolve around estate planning and the rights you have on behalf of your spouse. Some of them also have to do with the right to bring a lawsuit in the event of an injury, and others have to do with criminal behavior. Fortunately, I didn't and haven't had to avail myself of any of these benefits.

There are significant gift and estate tax benefits, even if there are still some income tax detriments (the "marriage tax.") Married couples can make unlimited lifetime gifts to each other - this means you aren't limited to the current annual gift exclusion.

In addition, you can leave your spouse an unlimited amount of assets at your death without any estate taxation. I used to call this the "Bill Gates" deduction, but now that he and Melinda have split, I need to come up with another name - the "Jeff Bezos" deduction - no, he's not married anymore either. How about the "Elon Musk" deduction - nope, not married either. I'm running out of candidates. Suffice to say that if you are married to a U.S. citizen, you can transfer an unlimited amount of assets during life or at death without a gift or estate tax consequence.

5 Make unintentional "taxable" gifts.

Married couples can make lifetime and at death gifts in unlimited amounts. This is true if you are married to a U.S. citizen. Regardless of your commitment to the relationship, the law treats you as a virtual stranger if you are unmarried.

For gift tax purposes, you are limited to annual gifts of the "annual exclusion amount." These are gifts you can make to as many people as you like without reporting them to the Internal Revenue Service (IRS). The amount can change annually and may be adjusted for inflation.

Suppose you and your partner own an asset jointly, and one partner contributes more than half of the expenses or value to that property annually. In that case, there may be an unintentional transfer of assets for gift tax purposes. If this amount exceeds the annual exclusion amount, the gift must be reported to the IRS and deducted from your lifetime gifting limit.

If you are "giving" assets to your partner annually and those gifts exceed the annual exclusion amount, then these are also reportable gifts. It is not too difficult to fall into this trap, so beware.

For estate tax purposes, you can leave an unlimited amount of money to your U.S. citizen spouse at the time of your death without any estate tax consequence. And, unlimited means unlimited. It doesn't matter how much you leave to your spouse; there is no estate tax due at the first spouse's death. The IRS is patiently waiting for the surviving spouse to die.

However, if you are not married, you do not have this "unlimited" benefit. You are restricted to the amount considered to be the lifetime exemption amount before an estate tax is due. When the estate tax exemption was lower, this was more of a problem. Today, most couples will not have an "estate tax problem," but times they are a-changing.

Another trap for the unwary is the failure to claim the unused estate tax exemption of the first spouse to die. Of course, you have to be married to qualify for this benefit. (See Tip 28 for more information on the DSUE).

CHAPTER FIVE

Tips for Married Couples

This section is for married persons, regardless of the length of the marriage. The law differentiates between single and married persons. Theoretically (and likely, practically), a married person has significantly more rights related to another person than a single person will ever have. As a result, because the law attempts to protect married persons in ways it does not protect single persons, you may discover there are lots of laws you may not be aware of that can have both positive and negative effects on your estate.

1 Fail to get a prenuptial agreement in a second or more marriage.

A prenuptial agreement may not sound like the most romantic way to begin a new marriage. Still, these legal instruments can provide a lot of protection and save many heartaches if the relationship should terminate, either by death or by divorce. For older couples, a prenuptial agreement may have more to do with protecting the assets each person brings to the marriage to benefit the children from the previous marriage and provide protection for long-term care.

Many states prevent spouses from disinheriting each other without their permission. This is one function of a prenuptial agreement; to waive the statutory rights a spouse may have. Why do this? Lots of reasons. You and your new spouse may be similarly situated financially. Or, you may not be similarly situated financially. Each of you may have children from previous relationships. You may want to avoid unnecessary entanglements with your spouse's children if your spouse dies first.

When my father died, his trust-based estate plan included a provision that required my mother to get a prenuptial agreement in the event of her remarriage. This was not to penalize her or to discourage her from remarrying; it was to protect the assets she brought to the marriage for the benefit of her children. My mother remarried eight (8) months after my father died. She and her soon-to-be new husband, Ken, each agreed to get a prenuptial agreement. When Ken died five (5) years later, his children received his entire estate, exactly as it should have been.

I received a call recently from a family who just lost their mother. It was a sad story. She had married a man four years earlier who had Parkinson's disease, and she took care of him. He was estranged from his daughter.

As sometimes happens, the caregiver spouse dies first. That's what happened here. Her kids took great pains to tell me how their mother brought all the assets to the marriage and spent all of her time caring for her husband. He had always indicated he didn't want anything from her.

You can imagine their shock when I had to tell them that

although I was very sorry for their loss, and their mother was very kind to care for her ailing husband, none of it made a difference regarding the husband's rights as a surviving spouse.

The couple did not get a prenuptial agreement. State law provides he has an interest in her homestead property and all of her worldwide assets. That includes the family home left by her first husband and intended to pass to his children. And, guess who is back on the scene? The missing daughter of the man with Parkinson's, who now holds her father's power of attorney and is asserting his rights to his interest in his deceased spouse's estate. Oops. Certainly not the result they expected.

In the event of a divorce, a prenuptial agreement is essentially a written marital settlement agreement, prepared in advance. It outlines the assets each party is bringing to the marriage and will generally provide that each party waives the right to the assets of the other, including alimony. It may also address how the family home will be distributed - a situation that may arise if one of the parties owns the house before the marriage.

Most state laws do not allow a waiver of child support. Child support is a parental obligation that is non-waivable and is generally determined by the court or by statute. The entitlement to child support belongs to the minor children, not to the spouse.

A prenuptial agreement should be signed at least thirty (30) days before the marriage to have the greatest likelihood of success. Agreements executed too close to the marriage date may fail due to undue influence or coercion.

Each party should fully disclose all assets and liabilities so there is transparency as to the value of the estate that is being negotiated. This is especially important when the parties are not similarly situated financially or when one party has significant debts.

Each party should have their own counsel. It is not uncommon for couples to want to "rush" a prenuptial agreement and use the same attorney. This is not recommended. The interests of the parties are not the same and one attorney cannot adequately represent these adverse interests.

2 Separate without ever getting a divorce.

It is not uncommon for couples to separate and then never get divorced. They live separately. They lead separate lives. Yet, they have never dissolved their marital relationship. If you never get divorced, then your spouse is still your spouse for all legal purposes.

If you die without a Last Will, your spouse will likely be your primary heir. Your spouse will have preference to be appointed as the administrator of your estate or as your guardian or to make healthcare-related decisions for you. Think long and hard before you neglect to terminate your legal marital relationship with someone you no longer have a relationship with.

Sometimes people stay together "for the sake of the children" or because the unknowns associated with the divorce process are too intimidating. Don't be penny-wise and pound-foolish. If you no longer want to be in a legal relationship with someone, get a divorce. The other option is to hope you live longer than your spouse. But remember, hope is not a plan.

3 Ignore state laws that affect your marriage and the distribution of assets - e.g., intestacy, homestead, elective share.

Many people are unaware that the act of marriage conveys as many as 1,100 rights to your spouse, something I call the unexpected wedding gift. We don't have time to discuss all 1,100 rights but suffice to say that most are related to your assets.

There are state laws that ensure your spouse will have assets and/or a home if you die without providing for your spouse. Federal laws protect your spouse's interest in your retirement plan (e.g., 401k or anything governed by ERISA). There are federal laws that affect your right to Social Security benefits, military benefits, or pensions. Gift and estate tax laws are affected by your marital status. Preference laws for the appointment of estate administrators, guardians and surrogates favor spouses. Even criminal laws protect spouses from giving incriminating testimony against each other.

Before you get married, consider all of the possible outcomes of that legal arrangement. This is especially important if you are entering into your second or more marital relationship. It may be in your best interest to get a prenuptial agreement. Meet with a qualified legal professional before entering into a mostly permanent legal relationship without guidance.

4 Assume your kids and your spouse will get along after you die.

This one is almost laughable. If your spouse and your kids didn't get along when you were alive, they will definitely not be living happily ever after when you die. When people die, relationships are affected by money and things (personal property). Everyone wants their share, and some people want more than their fair share. Sadly, it's human nature.

The two most common questions at a funeral are, and the phrase is almost ALWAYS preceded by "I don't mean to be greedy but," 1. "What do I get?" and 2. "When do I get it?" When I attend a funeral, I sit back and wait for it....

When families fight, lawyers win. Always. One hundred percent of the time. Your goal should be to ensure that your family does not fight when you die. That means understanding the who, what, where, why, and how of your estate plan so that the results are exactly what you expect.

5 Disinherit your spouse without their consent.

Most state laws look unkindly upon a spouse that tries to disinherit their spouse. If you have a spouse, they likely have entitlements to all or a portion of your estate. If you try to change that without their permission, your estate will be buying a lawsuit. Did I mention that when families fight, lawyers win? Thought so.

If you want to disinherit your spouse for a legitimate estate planning or elder law planning reason, then get a prenuptial agreement before the marriage or a postnuptial agreement after the marriage. Get legal representation because the laws are complex, and you will likely not be aware of all its nuances.

I can't speak to other states, but in Florida, a surviving spouse has a minimum entitlement to 30% of the deceased spouse's estate. This is their worldwide estate, not just their probate estate. Not just what's in their revocable trust. Not just their life insurance. Not just their retirement plan. EVERYTHING they own in the world. And, this includes assets owned jointly with others. Don't think you can just give it away during your lifetime, and that solves the problem. It probably won't because it looks and smells fishy.

The time to get permission to disinherit your spouse is before you marry them. Not after. I represent a lady whose husband owed their home before the marriage. They have now been married for more than 30 years, and he recently made it clear that when he dies, he doesn't want his spouse to have the house. He wants his son to have it. Fortunately for her, the law provides that he cannot transfer his homestead property or mortgage his homestead property without her consent. He also cannot leave it to his son without her consent. Ultimately, she gave her consent, and he wrote her a check for $100,000.

6 Forget to include remarriage protections - after the death of the first spouse.

Remarriage protections are those terms and conditions included in an estate plan that protect the surviving spouse in the event of remarriage. If I create a trust for my spouse's benefit, I can include some written provisions intended to protect my spouse and my family in the event of a remarriage after my death.

The trust for my spouse's benefit can suggest or require that he get a prenuptial agreement before entering into a subsequent marriage. I can't make my spouse protect his assets, but I can require that he protect the assets I'm leaving for his benefit. I can also prevent him from managing the assets left for his benefit if he fails to meet this requirement. I can require him to have a co-Trustee to manage the trust assets to ensure they are invested and spent wisely. Technically, I could limit his access to the income and/or principal of some of what I might leave for his benefit as well.

I like to call remarriage protections "Biff and Bambi protections." These protect your spouse in the event of a future remarriage. When I discuss this with clients, I always get a chuckle. One hundred percent of the time, a female spouse will say, "Hell NO, I'm never getting married again." A male spouse will just sit there quietly. It happens every time, and I just wait for it...

The reality is that lots of male people will remarry after the death or divorce of a spouse. And, lots of female people will, too - they just don't want to be too quick to admit to that fact.

7 Fail to notify an attorney after the death of your spouse - there's stuff to do.

When people die, there's stuff to do. There just is. Sorry. You need to file your spouse's Last Will with the relevant court. If you owned assets jointly, they will likely pass to the surviving spouse (you) by operation of law. However, you still have to provide a death certificate to the relevant financial organization for this transfer to be complete. For real property, you may have to record a death certificate or other supporting documents in the public records of each county where you own property. If you are the beneficiary of assets owned by your spouse, to claim those assets, you'll need to provide a claim form and a death certificate. If your spouse was receiving a pension, you'll need to notify the paying organization to determine if you have a right to ongoing payments. You might need to meet with Social Security. These are just a few examples.

You may need to cancel health insurance, car insurance, or other supplemental forms of insurance. You may need to cancel memberships in various organizations. You may need to transfer the ownership of vehicles owned by your spouse. The personal property of your spouse may need to be distributed to the designated beneficiaries.

Anything your spouse owns in their individual name that doesn't have a beneficiary designation will need to go through probate. If your spouse had a Last Will (the one you filed after your spouse died), it will set forth the terms and conditions of distributing your spouse's probate estate. If your spouse died intestate (without a Last Will), then the laws of your state will determine the proper beneficiaries for that asset.

If your spouse had debts at the time of their death, you may or may not be responsible for paying those debts. Technically, you are not responsible for the debts of your spouse unless: 1. You agreed to be responsible, or 2. You are the administrator of your spouse's estate, and there are sufficient estate assets to pay the legitimate creditor claims. Do not pay debts until you know whether you have a legal obligation to do so. Your moral obligation to pay your spouse's debts can always kick in later.

Some of this stuff might be easy, but some of it might be hard. Your legal counsel can advise you regarding exactly what you need to do.

8 Fail to update your estate plan during a divorce or immediately after that.

If you are getting a divorce (or you've already gotten one), you should consider updating your estate plan, reviewing your asset ownership, and revising all of your beneficiary designations. The last thing you want to do is die and accidentally leave stuff to the person you are trying to get away from or just divorced.

Some state laws provide a solution for divorced spouses. Some don't. In some states, when you get a divorce, all joint tenants with rights of survivorship relationships are severed, resulting in tenants in common ownership. Sometimes a former spouse in a life insurance policy, annuity contract, or retirement plan will be treated as if they had died, so there is no accidental receipt of benefits. In a Last Will or a Living Trust, your former spouse may also be treated as if they had died first.

Don't rely on the law to protect you; make sure you take the necessary steps to ensure that your assets and your estate plan reflect your current desires and wishes after your divorce.

Usually, it is a good idea to update your estate planning and begin retitling assets and renaming beneficiaries before the divorce is complete. Some courts, however, prohibit making any changes until the divorce is final. You need to know what the rules are in your jurisdiction.

When the divorce is final, you should review your estate plan, top to bottom, review all assets, check all beneficiary designations. Leave no stone unturned to ensure your plan is consistent with your goals. Sometimes, there are good reasons to continue to have your former spouse as a beneficiary. Sometimes your marital settlement agreement will require that you maintain life insurance or provide other benefits to a surviving spouse.

If you have a desire or a directive to provide for a former spouse, check with your legal counsel to make sure you've done it correctly. If your old Last Will provides for your former spouse and you still want them as a beneficiary, the best practice is to execute a new Last Will confirming your intention, so there is no mistake. The same is true for beneficiary designations. Even if you sign a form that renames your former spouse as the primary beneficiary, better safe than sorry.

CHAPTER SIX

Tips for Seniors

This section is for persons I'll refer to as Seniors - it doesn't mean you are old, but you are likely over the age of 60 and might be receiving Social Security as a form of income. Your estate planning needs will change as you age. You may move from traditional estate planning tools to those that fall into the category of "elder law" planning tools or legal strategies intended to preserve assets for the possibility you may need long-term care in the future. You will likely be retired from your primary career at this stage, even though you may still be employed.

1 Rely on social security as your only source of income.
If you think people don't do this, then you'll be surprised. I don't know anyone who can live any kind of lifestyle with Social Security as their only source of support. My mother-in-law tried. As a result, she lived in low-income housing for seniors. She

couldn't afford her car or insurance for it. All of her income went for food, internet, cable, and phone. There was nothing left over for vacations, travel, gift-giving, etc.

The only good news here is that when she found herself in a nursing home, she didn't have many assets to plan for and easily became eligible for Medicaid benefits.

2 Believe or expect the government will provide for your long-term care.

One of the most widely held myths is that Medicare will pay for long-term care in a nursing home or assisted living facility. Nothing could be further from the truth. Medicare pays for short-term rehabilitation. If you are not eligible or you use up your eligibility, that's it. No more Medicare. You private pay - either you or someone in your family. Your long-term care insurance pays. You go on Medicaid. That's it. Those are the choices.

The U.S. government is not in the business of paying for long-term care through its Medicare program. Medicaid is the ONLY government program that provides for long-term care in a nursing home. There are very limited programs for Medicaid assistance in an assisted living facility or at home. All programs have asset limitations and income caps. Most people without the help of a qualified elder law attorney will ever figure out how to become eligible before spending all of their assets.

You are responsible for planning for your future long-term care. Yet, most people don't plan, or they wait too long to plan. Then you are in crisis mode, and the options are always less attractive and more expensive than if you had taken the time to plan in your forties, fifties, and sixties. Trying to plan for long-term care in your eighties and nineties is like trying to buy homeowner's insurance when the house is on fire.

3 Spend all of your assets before consulting with a qualified elder law attorney regarding asset protection for long-term care.

Medicaid is the only government source for assistance with long-term care costs. It is designed for people who have limited resources and lower incomes. The program expects that people will plan or pay for their own long-term care. There are both asset limitations and income caps.

Many people believe the only way to become eligible for Medicaid is first to spend all of your assets. Then when you are completely broke, you can make an application. This is not true. A qualified elder law attorney can provide you and your family with guidance regarding planning for long-term care. There are strategies that may allow you to preserve assets for your care and for the future benefit of your family.

There are two types of planning - preventative planning and crisis planning. Which do you think most people do? Right! Crisis planning every time. We wait until the worst possible thing can happen, and then we get serious about doing something about it.

I tell my clients I prefer to do preventative planning, but I'm an expert in crisis planning. If you or a loved one may face the need for long-term care in the future, the time for planning is now. It's not usually the assets or the income that pose the biggest challenge. It is the competency of the person who needs the planning, and it is the family dynamic.

To do proper planning, you need to be competent. You need to have the adequate mental capacity to sign valid legal documents.

You need to understand your planning options and choose the ones that are best for you. You need to be able to delegate legal, financial, and healthcare decision-making authority in the event your mental or physical health deteriorates, and others have to make decisions for you.

If you wait too long and no longer have the capacity to sign legal documents, the only other recourse is a traditional guardianship. This is a lawsuit your family files against you, you get to pay for it, and you lose. Guardianship is not the best option because now any planning that needs to be done has to be done under the supervision of and with the approval of a judge. If you think planning is expensive, try a guardianship. A guardianship lasts for the rest of your life and requires ongoing court supervision.

Your family dynamic will also play a part in the type of long-term care planning you can do. If everyone gets along and is on the same page, you'll have a much smoother planning process. If there is disagreement about what to do, how to do it, who should do it, etc., your options become really limited, and the costs will likely skyrocket. Not everyone is blessed with a harmonious family.

4 Fail to claim all of the benefits you are entitled to - including Veterans Benefits & Medicaid.

The government benefits puzzle can be overwhelming. There's Supplemental Security Income (SSI), Social Security Disability Income (SSDI), Social Security Retirement Income, Medicare, and Medicaid. Then there are spousal benefits, survivor benefits, and disabled adult child benefits. If you are a veteran, you may also be eligible for certain Veterans Affairs (VA) benefits. You can visit SSA.gov and try to navigate all the various governmental programs. Good luck. Even the professionals have a hard time keeping it all straight.

One of my favorite sayings when it comes to calling Social Security or the Internal Revenue Service is, "If you don't like the answer, call back. You'll likely get another one." As a result, it's clear that even the people that work for these organizations don't know what's what.

5 Fail to create advance directives - with specific instructions regarding your end-of-life care.

Advance directives appoint and inform those you trust to handle your medical care decisions and your end-of-life wishes. The people you select should know you well enough to make decisions consistent with your wishes and beliefs.

A Healthcare Power of Attorney appoints a surrogate decision-maker for everyday medical care decisions. These would include consent to surgery, consent to treatment, transfer to or from a medical facility, release of medical records, the hiring and firing of caregivers and healthcare professionals, just to name a few.

A Living Will is your end-of-life declaration and sets forth the terms and conditions under which you would not want your life to be prolonged through the use of artificial means, including respiration, hydration, and nutrition. The individuals you nominate here are typically not making your decision; they carry out the written instructions you've left.

Sometimes, I'll have a client that wants the opposite of a Living Will. I call these a Will to Live. These individuals are adamant they want all medical measures taken to prolong their life, regardless of the circumstances.

Without a written direction, the law of your jurisdiction will determine whether you are maintained or removed from life support. A famous case that brought the need for advance directives to the national news is that of Terri Schiavo, who had no written instructions and her family engaged in a multi-year battle while she was maintained on life support. Her parents and her husband disagreed on whether she would desire to have life-prolonging interventions.

6 Choose the wrong Medicare supplement.

Medicare pays for medical care for individuals over age 65 and individuals under age 65 who are disabled. However, like most health insurance programs, Medicare does not pay for everything. You can purchase a Medicare supplement to pick up copays and pay for some of the medical services that Medicare doesn't pay for.

Like all insurance policies, some are feature-rich, and some are bare bones. If you don't have the right Medicare supplement, you may discover the error of your ways at a time when you can least afford it.

Find and develop a relationship with a professional who is skilled in the world of Medicare and Medicare supplements so you can make informed decisions.

7 Fail to plan for your burial, cremation, memorial.

If you fail to plan for your burial, cremation, and/or memorial, then your family and friends will be making those decisions for you. If you have not expressed your wishes, then people can only guess what you might have wanted.

Not everyone wants to be buried. The costs can be substantial. Not everyone wants to be cremated. Some may have religious beliefs that may prohibit cremation. Cremation is typically a more cost-effective option for final disposition.

A funeral or a memorial can be a somber affair or a celebration of an individual's life and accomplishments. You can be as creative as you like so that your day of remembrance is a true reflection of the extraordinary life you lived.

8 Fail to have expanded elder law powers in your power of attorney for long-term care planning.

Estate planning and elder law are not the same things. They share many of the same principles, but elder law focuses on that part of an individual's life when they may be aging and may face a future mental disability. You may also face a short or long-term stay in a rehabilitation facility or long-term nursing home facility.

Your family may need to implement elder law planning tools to preserve and enhance your estate for long-term care asset protection purposes. If you cannot make these decisions for yourself, then another may have to make them for you. To act without the supervision of the guardianship court, you will need a Durable Financial Power of Attorney with expanded elder law provisions that allow your nominee to engage in planning on your behalf.

Many traditional powers of attorney may not contain the elder law provisions necessary to implement a comprehensive long-term care asset protection plan for you. They will need the authority to create trusts on your behalf; this may include Medicaid Asset Protection Trusts, Qualified Income Trusts, or Special Needs Trusts. They will need the ability to liquidate assets, change beneficiary designations, resign you from fiduciary positions and make gifts on your behalf, just to name a few.

As you age, enter into a conversation with a trusted elder law attorney who can provide you with proper guidance regarding the appropriate estate planning and elder law tools.

9 Fail to include gifting powers in your power of attorney. A common long-term care asset protection planning tool is gifting. If you cannot afford the cost of your long-term care, it may be prudent to consider a long-term gifting program where you would make gifts either outright or to an asset protection trust. If you are unable to make these gifts yourself, then your nominated agent in a Durable Financial Power of Attorney needs to have the requisite gifting powers to make these gifts for you.

There may also be a need to give gifting powers if you have a significant estate that may be subject to estate tax. If you lose your mental capacity, your nominated agent may want to implement some gifting strategies that would reduce your estate's exposure to estate tax, currently 40%. Be wary of do-it-yourself gifting. If an agent makes gifts on your behalf, it should likely be part of an overall, coordinated, comprehensive estate tax or Medicaid plan.

Many "off the shelf" powers of attorney lack many of the sophisticated planning provisions that would be common for skilled estate planning and elder law attorneys to use as part of their toolset.

Remember, if you cannot make your own decisions and have not sufficiently delegated the powers necessary to provide proper planning, then the only other alternative is the guardianship court. Your guardian would then need to explain each of the necessary strategies to a judge who may not fully comprehend how each method may benefit you and your family.

CHAPTER SEVEN

Tips for Pet Parents

This section is for those persons who consider themselves to have "children who wear fur coats." You are the pet lovers of the world that know your pets deserve the same consideration in your estate planning that your children with two legs deserve. Our children who wear fur coats love us unconditionally but have limited legal rights. Our job as devoted pet parents is to ensure we have an estate plan that considers their lifetime needs. No loved pet should ever end up homeless or in a shelter. Yet, the statistics are grim - it is estimated that 500,000 loved pets are euthanized annually because their pet parent didn't have an estate plan that contemplated the long-term care needs of their pets.

1 Fail to create a plan that provides for the lifetime love and care of your pet.

You love your pet like family (and sometimes even more than your two-legged family members.) You would never do anything to harm your pet. However, if you do not have an estate plan that includes a comprehensive plan for your pet, your pet may become a statistic. It is estimated that more than 500,000 loved pets are euthanized each year because their pet parent didn't have a plan that detailed how the pet was to be cared for and the resources to provide that care.

Pet Trusts are now valid in all 50 states and the District of Columbia. There is no excuse not to create a Pet Trust if you love your pet. Animal Care Trust USA, Inc., a national nonprofit organization, is dedicated to keeping loved pets in loving homes. They provide education, Pet Trusts, Pet Trustee services, and resources to pet parents who are serious about their pet's lifetime love and care. You can get more information at ACT4Pets.org.

Even if you don't create a Pet Trust for your pet, make sure you nominate several individuals who are willing and able to care for your pet. Leave them some money so the costs of care are covered. There are a lot of options for making sure your loved pet stays loved.

2 Assume your friends or family will love your pet as you do.

No one will ever love your pet as you do. Five hundred thousand loved pets are killed in shelters each year because a pet parent assumed their friends and family would care for their pet. Your pet doesn't deserve to become a statistic. Family and friends mean well. They may even tell you what you want to hear, but when push comes to shove, there is no guarantee they will love your pet.

You can create a Pet Trust to ensure your pet is loved and cared for. All 50 states and the District of Columbia have enacted laws that allow a pet to be a beneficiary of a trust created for their lifetime care.

You can hire your own attorney to create a Pet Trust, or you can work with a charity like Animal Care Trust USA to create a trust for your pet. A custom Pet Trust allows you to detail your care requirements for your pet, select your pet caregivers, select your Pet Trustee and name your final beneficiaries when the purpose of the Pet Trust is complete.

Animal Care Trust USA offers several Pet Trust options. You can join the ACT4Pets Community Pet Trust, their most affordable option. Your pet will be rehomed with a loving family or placed in a sanctuary.

You can purchase and personalize their Forever Loved Pet Trust and select your own pet caregivers and Pet Trustees. Another option is to empower Animal Care Trust USA to place your pet with a loving family or sanctuary and act as a Pet Trustee. Either way, you make the decision that is in the best interest of your pet.

You can learn more about Pet Trusts at Animal Care Trust USA, or you can read my book, *All My Children Wear Fur Coats - How to Leave a Legacy for Your Pet,* available on Amazon.

3 Make an outright distribution of your pet - with or without money.

Some pet parents will use their Last Will or Living Trust to make a specific gift of their pet to a named pet caregiver. Sometimes they leave money for assisting the pet caregiver with the lifetime care costs of the pet.

An outright gift of a pet provides no guarantees that your pet will be cared for. There's no Pet Trustee to ensure that the life you envision for your pet when you're gone actually happens. And, if you leave money along with your pet, there's no guarantee the individual won't simply keep the money and take the pet to the nearest animal shelter.

Shelters have come a long way in the last few decades, but we still euthanize more than 3 million healthy adoptable pets each year in this country. If you want to make sure your pet is loved and cared for, get a Pet Trust.

I can share horror stories of pets that ended up homeless and living on the streets because the children of the deceased didn't want the pet and simply let it out the back door. Every day there are hundreds of posts on social media asking for homes for pets when a pet parent dies or ends up in a nursing home. There's no excuse not to protect your pet.

4 Name your pet as a beneficiary of your Will.
The law still considers a pet to be personal property. You can't give a gift of money to your pet as an outright beneficiary. That would be the legal equivalent of leaving money to a chair or a table. The gift is invalid and will not be honored. The only way to leave money for the benefit of a pet is with a Pet Trust. Do I sound like a broken record yet?

Most people assume their pets will die before they do. Sometimes that's true. But true pet lovers will get another pet, and there will likely be a pet living in their home at the time of their death. And it isn't only the death of a pet parent that can make a pet homeless. What happens to the pet if the pet parent ends up in a nursing home or has to go to an assisted living that doesn't allow pets? It happens every single day, 365 days a year, year in and year out. Life happens fast. Plan for your pets like they are little children that will never grow up. They deserve to be protected.

5 **Use a Will as the vehicle to create a Pet Trust for your pet.**
Okay, I've convinced you to create a Pet Trust. Good for you. Now, don't put that Pet Trust in a Last Will. Wills require probate. Probate can be a slow, time-consuming process. Your pet can't wait for your estate to go through probate to have the resources and care it needs today.

A favorite client of mine created a Pet Trust as part of his Last Will. It took more than four months to get a Personal Representative appointed for his estate. Meanwhile, his five cats had to rely on the mercy and good intentions of his neighbors. Thankfully, they were willing to provide this care, and not just turn the cats out on the street or drop them off at a shelter. Lesson learned. Don't create a testamentary Pet Trust in a Last Will - if you do your pet's life will be at risk.

You can learn more about how to protect your pet with a Pet Trust by reading *All My Children Wear Fur Coats - How to Leave a Legacy for Your Pet.*

6 **Neglect to leave any or enough money to provide for the care of your pets.**
Pets cost money. They eat. They get sick. They need medical care. They need grooming. They need an annual check-up. They need flea and tick treatment. They need heartworm treatment. They need immunizations. If you have horses, they need a lot more stuff, including regular hoof care. They need a roof over their heads. They need daycare. They need a pet sitter when you travel. They have a lot of needs.

Even if your best friend in the whole wide world is willing to take on the responsibility for the day-to-day care of your pet, you need to provide enough money for the pet's lifetime care. It is unreasonable to assume that your friend is also willing to spend their money to care for your pet when you can leave money for that purpose.

It's a math problem. If you spend $100 a month to care for your pet, that's $1,200 per year. Multiply that number by the number of years your pet might live, and you have the total cost of pet care. Only don't forget to consider that your pet might live an unusually long life or that your pet may need emergency care or suffer from a chronic disease. There are lots of variables. It is always better to err on the side of leaving too much money for the care of your pet than not leaving enough.

I'm leaving my whole estate for the lifetime care of my pets. I want my pets to live in my home with a pet caregiver that moves in with them. I want them to have the same life without me that they would have with me. I have life insurance, savings, and investments that can be used for their care. No one will provide for my pets as I will. They are my responsibility. I adopted them. I brought them into my home. By doing so, I committed to providing for them for the rest of their lives. If I'm dead, who needs my money more than they do? No one. At least not until they don't need it anymore. Then the people I love can have what's left. The people can wait. If I'm gone, my pets will need care now.

You don't have to leave your whole estate to provide for your pets. You can. Some will. But at least figure out how much is more than enough to provide for your pets in the style to which they have become accustomed.

Leona Helmsley (the "Queen of Mean") left 12 million dollars for her dog, Trouble. Unfortunately, a judge decided that $12 million was too much for a dog and reduced the amount to $1 million. I completely disagree with this outcome. It was her money and her dog. If she wanted to leave $100 million to her dog, that should be her choice. Not some stranger (the judge) who doesn't love Trouble as Leona did.

7 Name individuals as the remainder beneficiaries of a Pet Trust.

I really don't think people make good remainder beneficiaries for a Pet Trust for the same reason I mentioned Leona Helmsley above. It was people who brought it to the judge's attention that she left $12 million to her dog. Likely because they wanted the money and didn't want the dog to have it.

Name a person as the remainder beneficiary of a Pet Trust, and you may find they won't have the patience to wait until the pets are done with it. Then there's a lawsuit, and the lawyers end up with too much of the money intended for the pets. Name a charity; they make much better beneficiaries and are a whole lot less likely to challenge the money left for the benefit of the pets.

8 Choose the wrong Pet Caregivers.

Choosing the wrong Pet Caregiver is like choosing the wrong babysitter for your kids. Bad things can happen. You aren't there to know how your "children who wear fur coats" are being cared for. Be very careful in your selection. Have one or more backup choices in case the first choice doesn't work out for any reason. People tell me all the time, "I know my family/friend will care for my pet." No, you don't. Things can change fast in a person's life, and you cannot predict how that will affect their ability or willingness to take care of YOUR pet.

Well-meaning, and I'm sure halfway decent people leave loved pets at shelters every single day for some of the stupidest reasons.

They are moving. They are having a baby. They changed jobs. They don't have time for their pet. I've never once heard someone give up a child for the same reasons. These are people that should never have gotten a pet in the first place. Pets have feelings, and they suffer when they are abandoned by the people they thought loved them. If you don't believe me, go to a shelter and see how terrified they are. Their fate is very uncertain and can include death.

A plan for your pet should be designed to ensure they will always have someone who will love and care for them. They might not have you, so choose more than one person, and at least one organization as a final choice that you know will be committed to the very best interest of your pet.

9 Choose the wrong Pet Trustee.

Your pet caregiver provides day-to-day care for your pet. Your Pet Trustee manages, administers, and distributes the money you've left for the lifetime care of your pet. Choose the wrong Pet Trustee, and your pet may not have the resources it needs for lifetime care.

Your pet caregiver should likely not also be your Pet Trustee unless you have a lot of confidence in them. Most of the time, this solution is the equivalent of just leaving money outright to your pet caregiver. There is no system of checks and balances. There needs to be someone (preferably an organization) acting in a fiduciary role that has the ability and the knowledge to ensure the money you've left is used for its proper purpose - the care of your pet.

Banks and trust companies have been providing fiduciary trust services for hundreds of years. They know what to do and how to do it. The problem with pets is trust companies have substantial minimums ($1 million is not uncommon), and those minimums may be significantly more than you are willing or able to leave for the care of your pet.

Animal Care Trust USA is the nation's only nonprofit organization willing to act as Pet Trustee for a custom drafted and funded Pet Trust. They also offer Pet Trust options with very reasonable minimum funding requirements depending on the level of care desired by the pet parent for their loved pet. You can get more information at ACT4Pets.org.

CHAPTER EIGHT

Tips for Families With Special Needs

This section is for families with one or more members who have a disability or fall into the category of special needs. A person with special needs can be someone with a learning disability or someone who requires 24/7 round-the-clock medical care. This section primarily focuses on the needs of persons who, as a result of their disability, cannot or should not be making personal, financial, and legal decisions. It also includes those persons who may be receiving government benefits - either SSI, SSDI, or Disabled Adult Child - and their family wants to ensure they will have sufficient resources and financial oversight to last a lifetime.

1 Fail to get a guardianship or guardian advocacy for your child when they turn 18.

When a person turns 18, the law treats that person as an adult capable of making personal and financial decisions. This is true even if the individual was born with or developed a disability before reaching the age of 18. Parents often assume that because they are the natural guardian and have provided the child with care up to this point, they will simply continue to do so.

The reality is that the age of 18 is a demarcation point for adulthood. If a parent wants and needs to continue to provide some or all of the decision-making for their child, they have to ask the court to name them as legal guardian. Some states offer a summary proceeding that may be referred to as guardian advocacy. Each state will have its own set of requirements for implementing a guardianship/guardian advocacy. Still, the outcome is essentially the same, the parent(s), a family member, or another qualified individual will become the legal and/or financial decision-maker for a person with a demonstrated disability.

Without the proper legal authority to make decisions on behalf of a young adult with a disability, that person may be vulnerable to exploitation. In the event of a medical crisis, the parent may be prevented from speaking or acting on behalf of this vulnerable person. I have observed insurance companies unwilling to talk to the parent of an adult person with a disability because the child is over 18, and the parent cannot prove they have this legal right.

2 Not knowing the difference between guardianship and guardian advocacy.

In states that offer both a guardianship and guardian advocacy option, it is important to know the difference and the reasons why one may be more appropriate than the other. Traditional guardianship typically requires a formal determination of mental incapacity.

On the other hand, guardian advocacy does not require a formal finding of mental incapacity but instead may rely on substantial medical evidence provided by the individual's primary care physician. In Florida, there are specific disabilities that the guardian advocacy process was designed to serve. This may also be true in other states and may include developmental delay, autism, cerebral palsy, or other childhood disabilities.

There are different types of guardianship. There is a guardian of the person who is responsible for making the day-to-day personal decisions on behalf of the person with a disability. This may also include determining where they will live, their social interactions, and their medical decisions. There is also a guardian of the property who is responsible for managing, investing, and distributing the financial assets belonging to the person with a disability. A plenary guardian is one that is appointed as both guardian of the person and guardian of the property.

Knowing what type of guardianship (person, property, or plenary) is appropriate for your child may result in lower overall costs and reduce the complexity of the process. In some states, a parent may represent themselves as the guardian advocate of the person. Most jurisdictions will require that legal counsel represent the person with the disability to prevent the possibility of exploitation and ensure the proper appointment of guardian/guardian advocate.

Divorced parents of a child with a disability may discover that visitation and child support orders continue into adulthood. Sometimes both parents want to continue as guardians on behalf of the child. This may or may not be a workable solution depending on the cooperation between the parents.

In all cases, it is advantageous to have one or more individuals identified as "standby guardians" if the nominated guardian is unable or unwilling to continue serving in that position. The appointment of a standby guardian allows for a smooth transition on behalf of the person with a disability.

Seek counsel from a qualified elder law attorney with experience in special needs to answer state-specific questions you may have in this regard. You can also read my book, *Special People, Special Planning - Creating a Safe Legal Haven for Families with Special Needs"*, available on Amazon.

3 Fail to create a Special Needs Trust to protect eligibility for government benefits.

Some government programs that benefit persons with special needs are means-tested. This means they have both income and asset limitations. A Special Needs Trust will likely be required for the person with special needs if they have access to resources that exceed these income and asset limitations. A Special Needs Trust can also protect assets received as an inheritance from parents or other family members.

Special Needs Trusts come in two varieties (with variations within each type) - First-Party Special Needs Trusts and Third-Party Special Needs Trusts. A First-Party Special Needs Trust is funded with the disabled person's own money and requires repayment to Medicaid. A Third-Party Special Needs Trust is funded with money from third parties (e.g. parents or other family members) and does not require Medicaid reimbursement. The requirement for Medicaid reimbursement (known as payback) is the distinguishing difference between the two types of Special Needs Trusts.

Proper special needs planning contemplates the differences between the two types of Special Needs Trusts. A Third-Party

Special Needs Trust - either a standby trust or a standalone trust - is recommended when parents or family are planning for the lifetime needs of a child with a disability in order to avoid the requirement of Medicaid payback.

An unexpected inheritance outside of a Special Needs Trust, a personal injury settlement, or another form of financial windfall may require a First-Party Special Needs Trust in order to maintain government benefits eligibility.

4 Not understanding the differences between SSI, Medicaid, SSDI, Medicare, and Disabled Adult Child benefits from Social Security.

These are the primary government benefit programs for persons with disabilities. Each has its own requirements for eligibility. Some are means-tested, and some are not. All require a basic understanding of their eligibility requirements and how they can benefit a person with special needs.

SSI (Supplemental Security Income) is a program designed for low-income individuals who are disabled and who do not have a sufficient work history to qualify for SSDI (Social Security Disability Income). Eligibility for SSI generally also qualifies an individual for Medicaid, a program that provides health-related benefits to recipients.

SSDI is a program designed for disabled individuals who have a work history and have paid into the Social Security system for a requisite period of time. To be eligible for SSDI, a person has to be unable to engage in substantial gainful activity. In other words, they are unable to work and make an income that meets the Social Security definition of substantial gainful activity. Receipt of SSDI for 24 months or having a "listed" disability entitles the recipient to Medicare, a program that provides health-related benefits.

A person may be dual eligible for SSI, Medicaid, SSDI, and Medicare in some instances. Confusing huh?

Adult disabled children of parents who are receiving SSDI, Social Security (after retirement), or after an eligible parent has died may be entitled to Disabled Adult Child benefits. Generally, the child's disability has to have begun prior to the age of 22 in order to be eligible.

5 **Not knowing and understanding the difference between First-Party and Third-Party Special Needs Trusts.**
A First-Party Special Needs Trust is referred to as a Medicaid payback trust. That means when the trust beneficiary dies, there is an obligation on behalf of the Trustee to notify Medicaid to ascertain whether there is an obligation to repay Medicaid for services provided to the beneficiary during their lifetime. This obligation to repay Medicaid can seriously impact the ability of other family members to benefit from remaining trust assets.

First-party trusts are required any time a person with a disability receives government benefits and does not want to lose them because they have acquired assets that put them over the asset/resource limitation for either SSI or Medicaid. First-party assets generally arise from a person receiving a personal injury award, unexpected outright inheritance, or other outright gifts such as life insurance or retirement plan benefits where the person with the disability was named as an individual beneficiary.

A Third-Party Special Needs Trust is created by someone other than the Special Needs Trust beneficiary with assets that do not belong to the beneficiary. They are gifts from someone else - either a parent, sibling, grandparent, or another person. These are gifts to a trust and are not gifts outright to the person with special needs. When properly drafted, the person with the disability can maintain their eligibility for means-tested government benefit programs.

Third-Party Special Needs Trusts do not require Medicaid payback. This makes them very attractive because it allows other family members to benefit from the assets remaining in the trust after the death of the person with special needs.

6 Choose the wrong Special Needs Trust Trustee.

It is not uncommon for parents or persons creating a Special Needs Trust to believe they will save money by appointing a friend or family to serve as the trustee. Unfortunately, this decision can be penny-wise and pound-foolish. Most family members are not equipped to make good decisions related to the investment, administration, and distribution of assets from a Special Needs Trust. There are just too many rules and regulations regarding how persons with disabilities can receive assets for most laypersons to be comfortable making these decisions.

All First-Party Special Needs Trusts are "sole benefit" trusts, and the trust's assets can only be used for the person with the disability. It is not uncommon to see family member trustees use the money from the Special Needs Trust for other family members, thus violating the terms of the trust and putting the Special Needs Trust beneficiary and their benefits at risk.

Corporate trustees, nonprofit organizations qualified to act as trustees, some attorneys, and some certified public accountants are a much better choice as trustees than a family member. These entities and individuals should have the requisite knowledge to keep the trust assets appropriately invested and not violate the distribution rules affecting government benefit eligibility. And, if they make a mistake, they generally have deep pockets, liability, or malpractice insurance to rectify any damage incurred.

7 Fail to learn about the different benefits available in your state for the benefit of your child - ie. Medwaiver, IEPs, etc.

Every state has programs designed to benefit individuals with special needs. These programs are not uniform from state to state. Each of these programs has its own eligibility requirements, wait-lists, and benefits. As the parent or advocate on behalf of a person with special needs, you must arm yourself with the knowledge of the programs available in your state or your county.

8 Move to another state and assume you'll get the same benefits.

The benefits available to persons with a disability can vary widely from state to state. Some states have robust programs, and others provide very few benefits. It is never a good idea to decide to move without investigating the benefits available in the new state before you pack the truck and head down the road. You could find there is a big surprise waiting for you at the other end.

And, just because you are eligible for benefits in your home state doesn't automatically mean you'll be eligible in the new state. There may be a waiting list for services or different eligibility criteria.

9 Move to another jurisdiction or state and assume you don't have to move your guardianship.

I recently met with a client who relocated to Florida from another state several years ago. I was surprised to learn they had a family member with a guardianship in their former state that had never been moved to Florida. It never occurred to them when they moved to seek a transfer of the guardianship at that time. Typically, a guardianship is established in the county where the ward (incapacitated person) resides. When that person moves to another jurisdiction, the court needs to be advised of the move. The court is the state's representative regarding the well-being of the person who is disabled. They are charged with the responsibility of monitoring the activities of both the guardian and the ward to ensure the ward is not being exploited and the guardian is acting in their best interests.

Most states require the guardian to file an annual guardianship report that notifies the court of the ward's daily activities, where they are living, what doctors they've seen and what the ward's future looks like. In addition, if there is a guardianship of the property, the guardian may be required to file an annual accounting with the court to advise how the ward's money and property are being spent and managed. Many guardianships require the guardian to get court approval for expenditures over a specific dollar amount.

If you are the guardian of another and you move, notify the court of the change in residence. You'll likely be required to transfer or establish the guardianship in the new jurisdiction where the ward will reside.

CHAPTER NINE

Tips for Business Owners

This section is for the entrepreneur/business owner and some of the unique concerns related to business ownership. In addition to having a personal, comprehensive foundational estate plan, the business owner will need an estate plan for their business interests. And, because your business is likely your largest asset, failing to create a plan that contemplates the legal and efficient transfer of this asset could have disastrous results - both financially and for the business's longevity.

1 **Fail to create a written succession plan, including a Buy-Sell Agreement.**

Starting a new business is an exciting adventure. There's so much to do and learn. Any time there is more than one owner of a business, the potential for future disagreement exists. This is especially true when it comes to the succession of the business if one of the owners is unable to continue for any reason. Typical reasons for inability to continue include disability, death, divorce, retirement, or personal bankruptcy. If the business owners have not discussed and then memorialized in a written agreement how the succession of the business will take place in the event of one of these "dissolution" issues, there could be trouble ahead.

A written succession agreement with clearly stated terms and conditions for the purchase and sale of the business and, specifically, your interest in the business (a Buy-Sell Agreement) can protect your business and your interest in the event of a "dissolution" event. Failure to do so will leave your business floundering and may end up costing thousands in attorneys' fees.

2 Fail to review the terms and conditions of your Buy-Sell Agreement annually.

Congratulations, you have a clearly written and comprehensive Buy-Sell Agreement that lays out all the terms and conditions for the purchase or sale of your business in a "dissolution" event. Now your job is to review that agreement annually to make sure the terms and conditions remain relevant to the current status of the business.

Many Buy-Sell Agreements establish a formula for calculating the value of the business if a purchase or sale is necessary. Others may establish a fixed price per share. The Buy-Sell Agreement should also establish the terms and conditions for any promissory notes that allow the "buying" owner to purchase the shares of the "departing" owner. These terms and conditions would include what portion of the purchase price could be financed, the loan's length, and the loan's interest rate.

I recently had a client who had been in business with her

partner for forty years. It was a family-owned business, but because of her long-term commitment to the company, she had been given one share of the company and the opportunity to buy the remaining five shares in the event of the death of her partner. The majority partner died, and the provisions of the Buy-Sell Agreement became relevant.

Amazingly, the partners reviewed the agreement annually to update the value of each share and the buy-out value of the company. What they failed to review was the terms and conditions of the promissory note. As a result, the "buying" partner was saddled with an above-market value interest rate (and considerably higher monthly payments) than she was comfortable with. There was also some misunderstanding about whether the son (who also worked in the business) would be entitled to become a future owner in the company.

Ultimately, it was settled that the son would not become an owner of the company until he invested more time and commitment to its success. The "buying" partner had to go out into the commercial lending marketplace to refinance the loan and pay off the spouse of her deceased partner.

There was a lot of unnecessary angst, attorneys' fees, and delays that could have been avoided had the partners done a more thorough annual review to make sure all of the terms and conditions of the Buy-Sell Agreement were consistent with the changing business landscape.

3 Forget or fail to buy life insurance to fund the buy-out provisions of your Buy-Sell Agreement.

A Buy-Sell Agreement sets out the terms and conditions under which a "departing" business owner will sell their shares in the company to the remaining owner(s). If the business is successful, the buy-out amount can be substantial, and the "buying" owner may not have liquid financial resources available for the purchase price. As a result, purchasing a life insurance policy may be the best way to raise cash to buy out the deceased owner's family or estate.

The problem with life insurance is that you can't get it when you need it, so you must plan ahead. Life insurance policies should be purchased when the owners are all young and healthy. The policies should be reviewed periodically to ensure they are sufficient in value to cover the purchase price. And, the purchase of "cheap" term insurance may not be appropriate because, at the end of the insurance policy term, the premiums may be unaffordable, and the insured may no longer qualify from a health perspective for purchasing a new, more extensive policy.

I remember an instance where three business partners each had a 1 million dollar policy to purchase their share in the business in the event of death. One partner had told his spouse, "You never have to worry; if something happens to me, there's a 1 million dollar policy on my life to buy my interest." This was the only life insurance policy on the man, and he relied on this value for the future security of his spouse. Unfortunately, at the time of his death, the value of the company had changed significantly. The construction industry was in a downward spiral, and the other two owners had to inject substantial amounts of personal capital into the company (in the form of loans) to keep the company solvent. When the company was valued after the owner's death, he actually owed the company money! His dream of leaving his wife $1 million was no longer a reality and was only a drop in the bucket toward his financial obligation to the company.

4 Fail to buy short-term and long-term disability insurance for yourself and your employees.

If you or a key employee becomes disabled, either for a short-term or long-term period, their absence may significantly impact your business and their livelihood. Disability insurance comes in different varieties with lots of bells and whistles. Some short-term policies cover pregnancy and maternity leave, allowing an employee to stay home during the first few months of a newborn's life.

Companies like Aflac and Liberty National offer individual plans that can be paid by the employee on a payroll deduction basis. Employers can also contribute to the cost of the insurance.

There are also group long-term disability programs that employers can offer and can be very affordable. Generally, a long-term disability policy will cover 60% of an individual's salary for a specific period of time. The income received may also be on a tax-advantaged basis. Some policies cover what is called "own occupation," and others require total disability and a complete inability to work.

5 Think you know what the value of your business is - either too little or too much.

Most business owners have no idea of the true value of their business. When asked, they will either say a value that is extraordinarily high because that is what they'd like to receive if they sold it or extraordinarily low because they believe it has no value without the business owner's participation.

There are lots of valuation methods for determining the value of a company. The one that should be used for your company may depend on your industry and how similar companies are valued.

Business appraisal is a recognized profession, and it is recommended you get a business appraisal from a credentialed appraiser.

If your company is growing, it may be good to have a "baseline" valuation for future reference. If you die, the value of your business will be included in your estate for estate tax purposes, and your business may be worth more than you think. The fair market value of an item is defined as what a willing buyer would pay a willing seller. Typically, the Internal Revenue Value for a business is based on the value the day before the owner died, not the day after.

6 Fail to have enough liquidity to pay any estate taxes that may be due at your death.

The value of your business is included in the value of your gross estate at the time of your death. If the value of your business causes your estate to be taxable because it exceeds the estate tax exemption limit at the time of your death, then the IRS will want to be paid. If most of your wealth is tied up in your business, your family may not have other liquid assets with which to pay the tax bill. Estate tax returns and estate taxes are due nine (9) months after the date of death.

You would not want your family to have to sell your business at fire-sale prices to raise the capital required to pay the estate taxes. Yet, this happens regularly. Life insurance is the best-leveraged play there is for creating liquidity at a death event. But, don't wait too long. You need to get life insurance when you don't need it.

7 Fail to consider the impact on your family if you die, and they need to rely on the cash flow from your business.

If you are the sole owner of your business, you must consider the impact that your absence could have on the viability of your business after your death or disability. You may be the heart and soul of your business. You are the primary contact person; you have the institutional knowledge. Your employees and your customers rely on you to make sure the business operates smoothly on a daily basis.

I know a business owner who runs a 10 million dollar a year construction company. He personally nets $3 million annually in W-2 wages and distributions. He employs several project managers and works with more than 125 subcontractors at any given time. However, if he were to die or become disabled, there is no one identified in his office that could step in and manage the business. It could take weeks or months for someone from the outside to come in and figure out how the company runs. In the meantime, no new business projects would be added to the pipeline, key staff may leave due to the uncertainty surrounding the business and their future, receivables and payables may fall behind or be overlooked. If the business needs to be sold after the owner's demise, it may only sell for the asset value of approximately $300,000.

That kind of decrease in value and cash flow will substantially impact the business owner's family and lifestyle. Suppose the business owner and his family are in the habit of consuming their annual income (as opposed to saving it). In that case, the financial stability of the family is subject to collapse.

A business continuity plan is different from a business succession plan entered into with business partners. A business continuity plan contemplates how the business will operate in the absence of the business owner so both the value of the business and the family of the business owner will be protected. If the business is a sole proprietorship, then if the business owner dies, theoretically, the business no longer exists. This happened recently to a client when her husband died. Fortunately, both she and her sons had been working in the business and were able to create a new limited liability company and continue its operation.

CHAPTER TEN

Tips for the Committed Cryonicist

This section is for the small but growing number of people that have adopted a worldview that includes cryopreservation (either of their whole body or their brain) for a time in the future when we may have the science and the technology to revive that person to a living state. My cryonics clients are very optimistic about the future - they have faith in a future where they will be revived and functioning. And, they want to craft a way to ensure they will have financial stability for that future.

1 Use Traditional Estate Planning to accomplish a very Non-Traditional Goal.

Planning for a future when you may be in biostasis (also known as cryostasis) with the prospect of a subsequent reanimation (revival) is a legal frontier that is still the wild west. No one that has decided to be a cryonics patient has ever been revived. As a result, there are a lot of legal unknowns. Traditional estate planning tools and techniques will likely not work for the committed cryonicist. Seek out a legal professional (and there aren't many) who practices in this type of cutting-edge estate planning. I can name exactly two other attorneys that I know are familiar with this type of planning.

In my practice, I have adopted a form of cryonics trust called the Personal Revival Trust™. The purpose of this trust is to hold assets after the legal death of the cryonicist until the individual is revived at some unknown future date, if ever.

There are many issues specific to the cryonicist who wants to preserve assets for the future. Some of these include family dynamics, preservation of assets for surviving family members and pets, the rule against perpetuities, no-contest clauses, just to name a few.

You can get more information on estate planning for cryonics in *The Cryonics Estate Planning Handbook - Maybe You Can Take It With You* by Rudi Hoffman and myself, Peggy R. Hoyt. The book is available on Amazon.

2 Fail to consider using life insurance to leverage financial liquidity - both to fund your cryopreservation and create wealth for your future.

Life insurance has been used for generations as a means of creating leveraged wealth. You pay premium dollars today toward a life insurance contract that will have a guaranteed death benefit in the future. This death benefit can be used for a myriad of estate planning purposes. You can use life insurance to defray estate taxes, to provide wealth for your family, to pay for your cryopreservation, and to ensure you have access to financial resources in the future upon reanimation.

Like the legal aspects of planning for cryonics, the life insurance products you may want to use are typically not those you can "buy off the shelf." As a result, working with a professional familiar with cryonics and the nuances of a life or annuity contract that can help you accomplish your goals is a must. Rudi Hoffman, CFP, CLU, ChFC, and the co-author of *The Cryonics Estate Planning Handbook,* holds the credentials and experience the committed cryonicist needs to plan for their future. You can find Rudi at RudiHoffman.com.

ABOUT THE AUTHOR

PEGGY R. HOYT, J.D., M.B.A.
Attorney
The Law Offices of Hoyt & Bryan, LLC

Peggy is a lifelong animal advocate, pet mom, author, and attorney. Before entering law school, her work experience includes time as a college recruiter, financial consultant, account executive, and chief financial officer. She is a founding partner of The Law Offices of Hoyt & Bryan. Peggy is dual board certified by the Florida Bar in Wills, Trusts, and Estates and Elder Law. She is the founder of

Animal Care Trust USA, Inc., a national nonprofit whose mission is to keep loved pets in loving homes by educating pet parents about the importance of Pet Trusts.

She practices in the areas of family wealth and legacy counseling, including trust and estate planning and administration, elder law, small business creation, succession and exit planning, real estate transactions, and animal law. In addition to her law degree, she holds a Florida real estate license. Peggy formerly held an NASD Series 7 license and life, health, and variable annuities licenses. She serves as a certified FINRA Arbitrator. Peggy was an adjunct professor of Animal Law with Barry University College of Law.

Peggy is the author of *All My Children Wear Fur Coats – How to Leave a Legacy to Your Pet*, an informative guide for pet owners who want to include their pets as part of their estate plans. She has co-authored numerous other titles, including *Special People, Special Planning – Creating a Safe Legal Haven for Families with Special Needs*; *Loving Without a License – An Estate Planning Survival Guide for Unmarried Couples and Same Sex Partners*; *A Matter of Trust – The Importance of Personal Instructions*; *Women in Transition – Navigating the Legal and Financial Challenges in Your Life*; *Like a Library Burning – Sharing and Saving a Lifetime of Stories*; *Thank Everybody for Everything! Grow your Life and Your Business with Gratitude*; *Gratitude Expressions - a Five Year Journal*; *Straight Talk! About Estate Planning*; *Straight Talk! What to Do When Someone Dies*; *What's the Deal With... Estate Planning* and *What's the Deal With...Estate Administration*. Her newest book with Rudi Hoffman addresses the estate planning concerns of cryonicists and is called, *The Cryonics Estate Planning Handbook - Maybe You Can Take it With You*. She was a contributing author to *Leading Counsel: Spotlights on Top Elder Law and Estate Planning Attorneys Vol. 2.*

Peggy frequently speaks on estate planning and elder law topics, including pet planning and planning for families with special needs. She has been featured on CNN Financial News, in the Wall Street Journal, and the Orlando Sentinel for her dedication to pet planning. She is also highly regarded for her workshops on gratitude marketing, life balance, and law office management. She hosts a weekly "Pawcast" called *All My Children Wear Fur Coats,* available on Buzzsprout.

Her educational background includes a B.B.A (Marketing/Management 1981), *cum laude* and M.B.A. (Finance 1982) from Stetson University. She received her law degree (J.D. 1983), *cum laude* from Stetson University College of Law. She is a member of numerous state and national organizations, including WealthCounsel and ElderCounsel, the Central Florida Estate Planning Council, the National Association of Elder Law Attorneys (NAELA), and the Academy of Florida Elder Law Attorneys (AFELA). She is active with The Florida Bar serving as a Past Chair for both the Solo and Small Firm Section and Animal Law Section. She is a member of the Elder Law Section and Real Property, Probate, and Trust Law Section.

WEBSITE: www.HoytBryan.com
PHONE: 407-977-8080
EMAIL: Peggy@HoytBryan.com
FACEBOOK: https://www.facebook.com/HoytandBryan
https://www.facebook.com/AnimalCareTrustUSA
LINKEDIN: https://www.linkedin.com/in/peggyrhoyt/

WHAT PEGGY'S CLIENTS ARE SAYING

"Peggy Hoyt is an outstanding attorney and person. Her legal expertise and timeliness in responding to our family's needs regarding estate state planning and business matters has been and continues to be invaluable. Peggy is a trusted advisor and friend. Thank You, Peggy."

-John, Shelia and Kaitlin H.

"My experience with Peggy Hoyt and her law firm is one of knowledge, competence and straightforward communication. You'll find the same in her new book. I recommend both her and the book highly."

-Casey F.

"We were referred to Peggy by our financial advisor in 2006. This proved to be one of the best things that could have happened to us as we found an excellent estate lawyer, a friend and confidant. Peggy has used her broad knowledge to keep us current on our trusts and all things affecting our family as we have grown our estate. Her relaxed demeanor has made it very easy to work with her and we look forward to maintaining this relationship."

-Bonnie B.

"I have known Peggy Hoyt for over 20 years. She has provided my clients and my family exceptional estate planning services during that time. She has encapsulated her knowledge and experience on this subject for all to read. If you are interested in protecting you, your family and your wealth and ensuring your plans for the future are realized, Read This Book!

-J. Michael Bass, CFP, CIMA

———

"I have known Peggy Hoyt for more than 25 years and she is one of my favorite trusted professionals! I am so fortunate to have crossed her path so long ago as I have always admired her and her practical approach to all matters legal and financial!! I would trust her implicitly as she has an incredible wealth of knowledge, a profound wisdom, and is full of integrity and candor we all love and appreciate so very much! You cannot go wrong trusting her to protect you and your loved ones' estates, including making sure your fur babies are cared for, after you are no longer able!"

-Karen R.

———

"Having owned and conducted business in the same area for 31 years, you come to know many professionals. I've never endorsed anybody as strongly as Peggy. She's the perfect blend of exacting professional excellence with down-to-earth compassion. I've referred my dearest clients, family, and friends to her, always to rave reviews. She's the type of person you'd trust with your life."
Enjoy the journey,

-Dan D.

Made in the USA
Columbia, SC
14 November 2022

71153697R00080